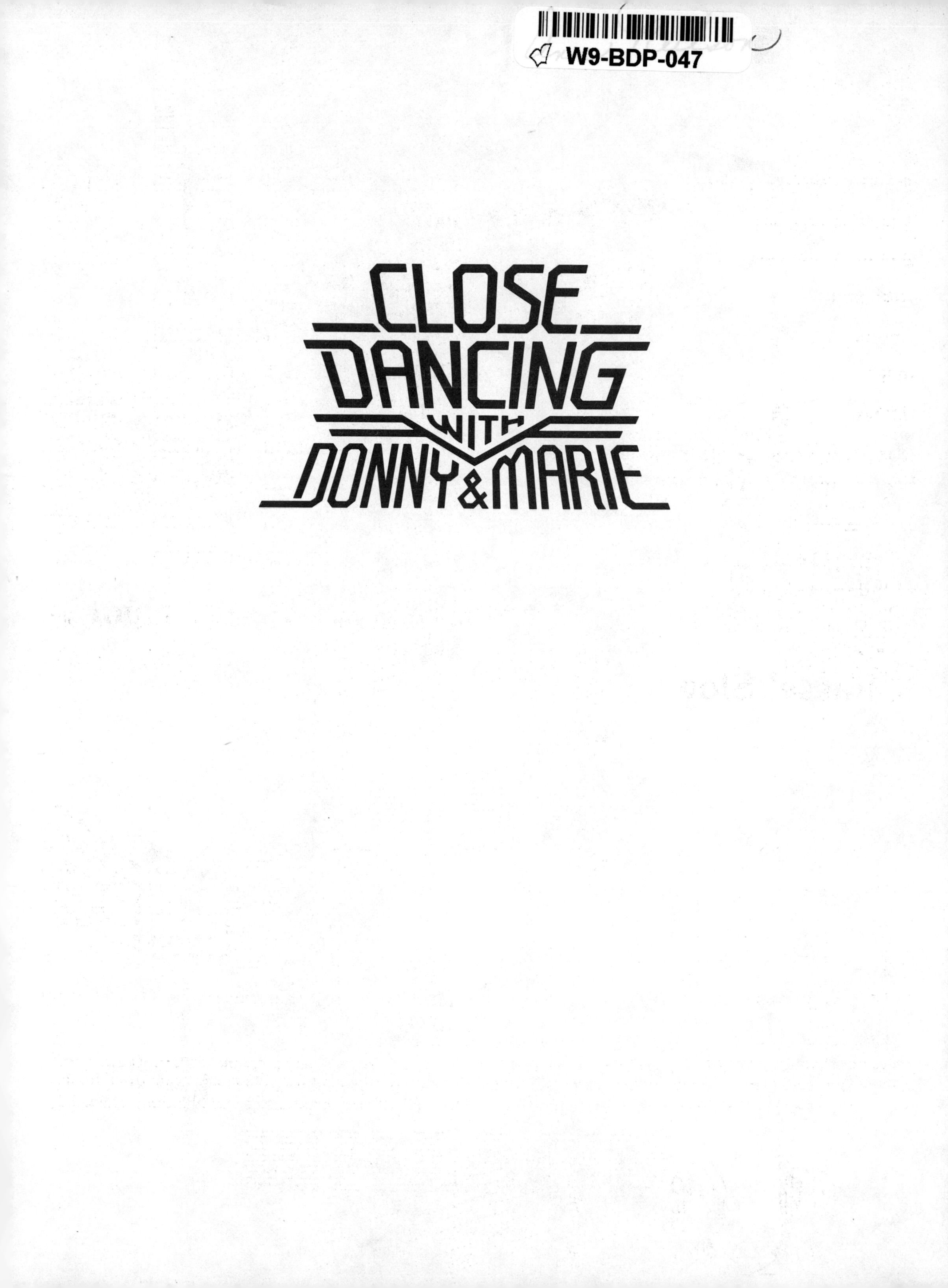
CLOSE
DANCING
WITH
DONNY & MARIE

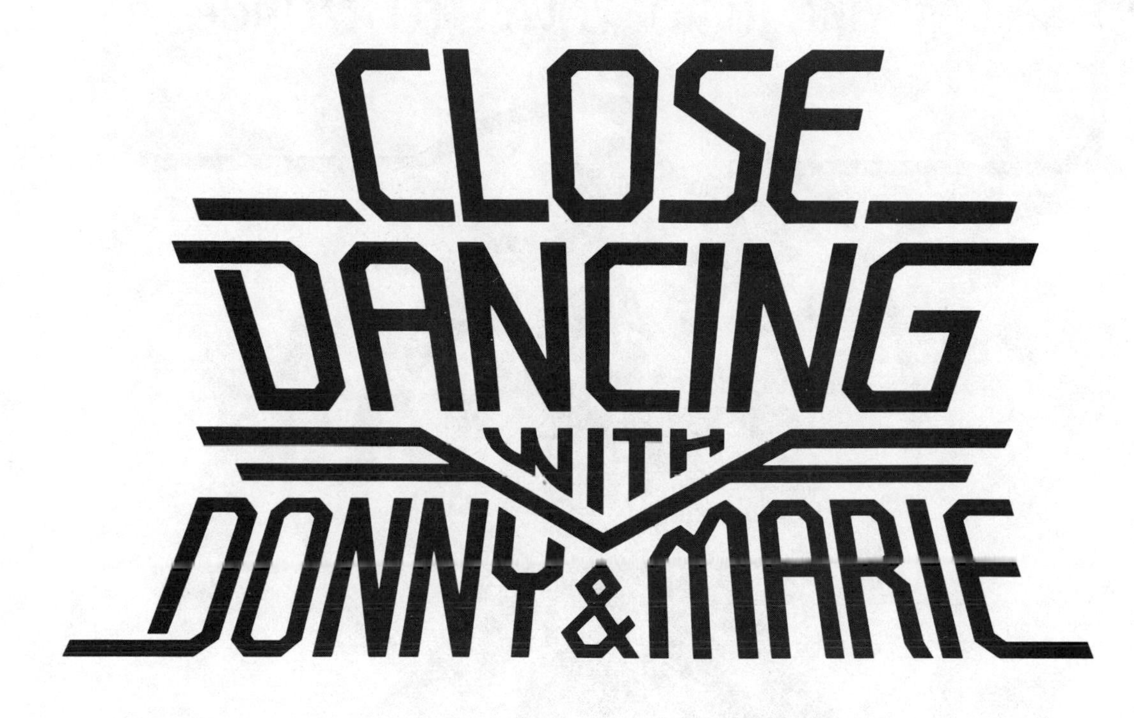

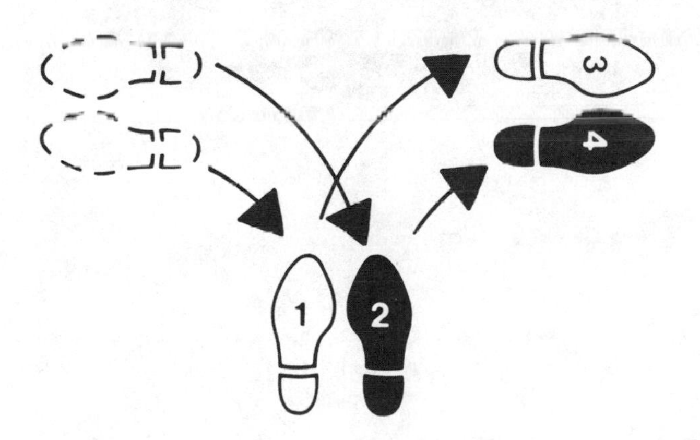

A Step by Step Guide To Ballroom Dancing

BY ALMA HEATON and DON ZIMMERMAN

PHOTOGRAPHY BY STAN MACBEAN
COVER PHOTO BY MITCHELL ROSE
DESIGNED BY GAYLA COLEMAN

THIS BOOK IS DEDICATED TO

I.S.B.N. 0-89888-001-7

Published in Utah by Osmond Publishing Co.

Library of Congress Card Number 79-87763

Printed in the United States of America

ACKNOWLEDGMENTS

The authors are indebted to the thousands of individuals who enjoy dancing and the many students that take social dancing each semester who have given of their time and talent to encourage the dance program.

Gratitude is expressed to photographer Stan Macbean, designer Gayla Coleman, and a special thanks to Donny, Marie, and Jay Osmond.

Thanks go to the Dance Masters of America, the American Education and Recreation for all the dance teachers who have given their instruction in teaching us how to dance.

The authors hope this book will be the stimuli for creating many happy hours of fun dancing.

CONTENTS

ABOUT THE AUTHORS

Alma Heaton and Don Zimmerman have had years of professional teaching experience. Both authors have a Bachelors degree in Professional Dance and Alma Heaton holds a Masters degree as well.

Alma Heaton has studied dancing from some of the top instructors in the United States and has had many years of professional teaching experience. The thesis for his master's degree was entitled, "The Techniques of Teaching Dancing." He has taught dancing at Weber State College, Utah State University, and Brigham Young University for over twenty five years, and he was technical director for five ballroom dance films. i.e. "Lets Dance," Techniques of Teaching Ballroom Dance," "Eight Basic Lessons, Foxtrot, Lindy, Waltz, and Cha-Cha Lessons," "How to Direct Social Activities," and "Family Recreation." He has also written numerous books on teaching dancing techniques.

Don Zimmerman has written, directed, choregraphed and performed in numerous musicals. A member of a select group of dance professionals, Mr. Zimmerman toured the world presenting a two-hour disco show for the United States Air Force. He is presently giving instruction in the Social Dance Program at Brigham Young University and owns his own dance studio in Provo, Utah ("The Dance Factory").

INTRODUCTION

There is a trend toward more precise and better structured methods of teaching ballroom dance. This book contains clear and well-organized descriptions of teaching techniques and learning methods presented in logical sequence.

The approach presented in this book to teaching ballroom dance makes it possible for the participant to learn a large number of variations from a few basic positions and basic step patterns. The material is presented in a way that makes ballroom dance enjoyable right from the first lesson.

Dancing is more than moving the feet in intricate patterns upon the dance floor. Contrary to the views of many people, skill in dancing and full enjoyment of this very popular leisure-time activity involves mastery of several important fundamentals. It is not enough to master the "Steps" alone; they must be danced in "rhythm" to the music, with the "styling" indicative of good dance form and suited to the type of music being played. The leader must be able to dance in other than the "closed position" if he wants freedom of expression in his dancing. Consequently, he must be able to "lead" his partner from step to step, rhythm to rhythm, position to posiiton around the floor without colliding with other dancers. Equally important, his partner must be able to "follow" through these various changes. All of this must be accomplished while maintaining good "posture," practicing desirable dancehall "etiquette," and in a happy, relaxed physical and mental condition.

Dancing is a popular leisure time activity enjoyed by young and old the world over. Those who learn to dance well tend to enjoy it more and continue their participation longer. Therefore, good instruction is basic to good performance and long-term enjoyment of dancing.

HOW TO USE THIS BOOK

Logical Sequence of Progression. The dances in this book are divided into two main categories: American Rhythms and Latin Rhythms. Every dance is broken down by dance rhythms; every dance rhythm is divided into lessons; every lesson is divided into step patterns. The book builds step by step, showing foot movements as well as weight changes, moving from simple to complex.

Step Descriptions. Beneath the diagrams in each dance lesson are abbreviated explanations of every step pattern. The first column, "Step," gives the name of the dance step. Column two "Position," gives the beginning position and indicates every time the partners change positions during a step pattern.

The "Directions" in column three are patterned after the dance rhythm, with capital letters for slow steps and lowercase letters for quick steps. Every optional step is converted into a forward, backward, or sideward step. Turning steps are underlined (______), and at the end of each line are braces ({}) with information regarding how far to turn in which direction. For example, "F CL F CL {tr 1/2}" means that you should turn right a ¼ turn on each forward step.

When the man and the lady do opposite footwork, as in closed position, or the same footwork, as in conversation position, only the man's part is given. When the man and the lady do different footwork, the lady's part is indicated by the symbol for the word "at," namely @. When only one partner turns, his or her step pattern is followed by braces (F F @ Fr B {tl 1/2}). When the man and the lady do the same footwork, but turn opposite directions, there are braces for each partner (Fr B {tr 1/2} {tl 1/2}). When they do opposite footwork, but turn the same direction, the information in braces applies to both partners
Fr B BK F {tr 1/2}).

Column four gives the "Hand Lead" for every step.

The best way to absorb each lesson is to run through every dance step several times--first counting the beats and then naming the dance steps, chanting the directions, and calling out the hand leads.
Diagrams. The man begins every step pattern with his left foot, and the lady begins every step pattern with her right. The man's starting position is indicated by a pair of dotted footprints with the word "man" above or below it; the lady's starting position is indicated by a pair of dotted footprints and the word "lady."

A step or weight change is shown by a solid footprint. (A) For the sake of deciphering the step patterns, the left foot is an outline and the right foot is solid. Solid arrows show regular foot movements and dotted arrows mean that beginning the step pattern from the starting position (or another dance) step is slightly different from repeating the same step pattern. The numbers inside each footprint show which foot movement corresponds to each beat of the music count. If the foot steps in the same place twice, the footprint contains two numbers.

A touch is shown by the toe of the footprint. (A) When a touch is followed by a hold, the beat of the music count appears where the heel would be.(B) When a foot moves back to the starting position, dotted footprints may be replaced by a step, (C) a touch, (D) or a touch and a hold. (E)

A draw is indicated by the beat of the music count instead of a footprint, and a kick is indicated by the beat of the music count with curved arrows drawn out and back in. (F) A progressive pivot is shown by overlapping footprints with the beat of the music count in the toe of the original step and a curved arrow to indicate the direction of the pivot. (G)

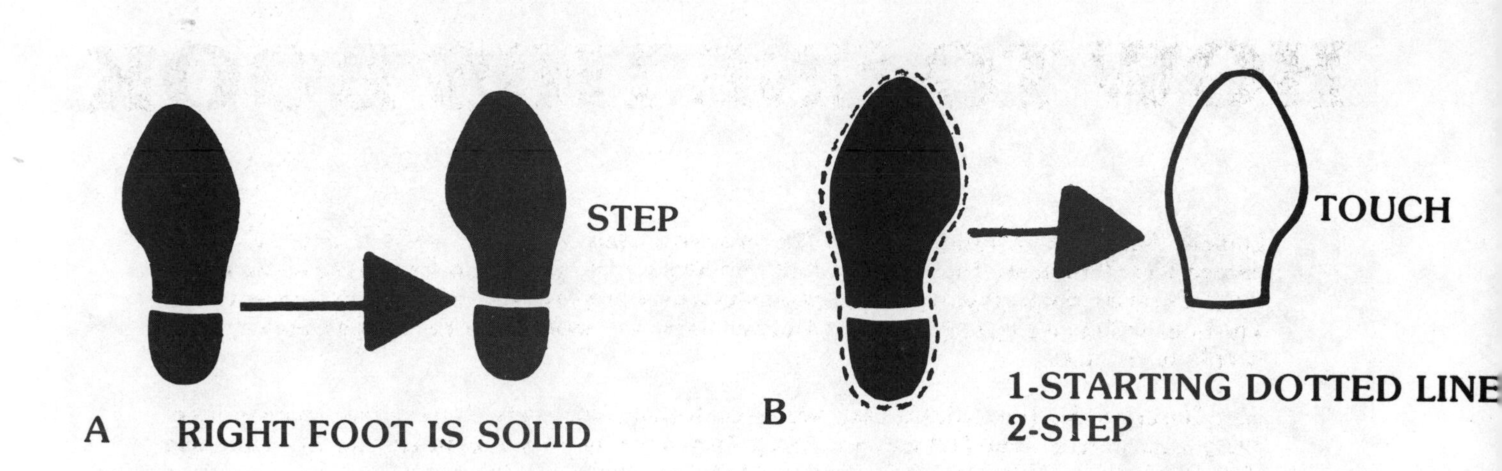

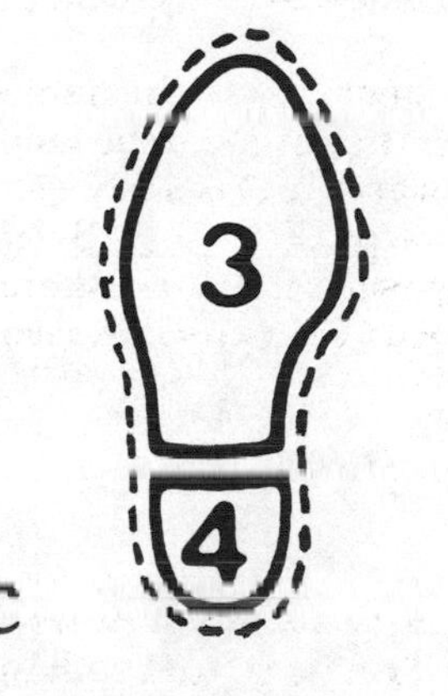

1-STARTING DOTTED LINE
2-STEP

1-STARTING DOTTED LINE
2-TOUCH OR HOLD

TOUCH AND HOLD

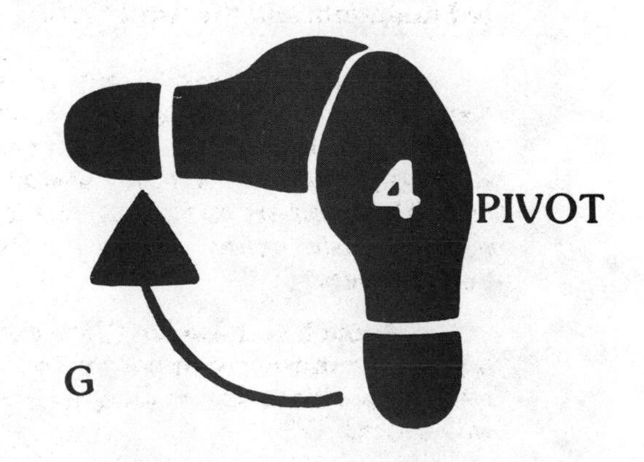

PART I

FUNDAMENTALS

Dancing is more than moving your feet with the music. To learn to dance well you must understand several basic concepts and master several fundamental skills. These concepts and skills may be learned most easily in the following order: Posture, Walking, Rhythm, Etiquette, Positions, Line of Dance, Foot Movement, Leading, Following, Steps, and Styling.

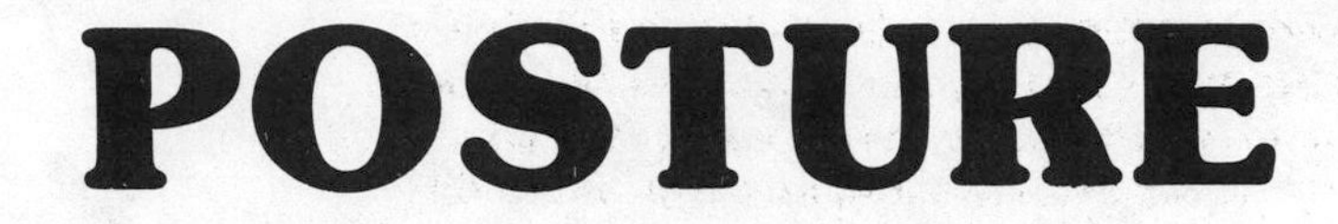

POSTURE

Dance posture refers to proper body carriage and alignment.

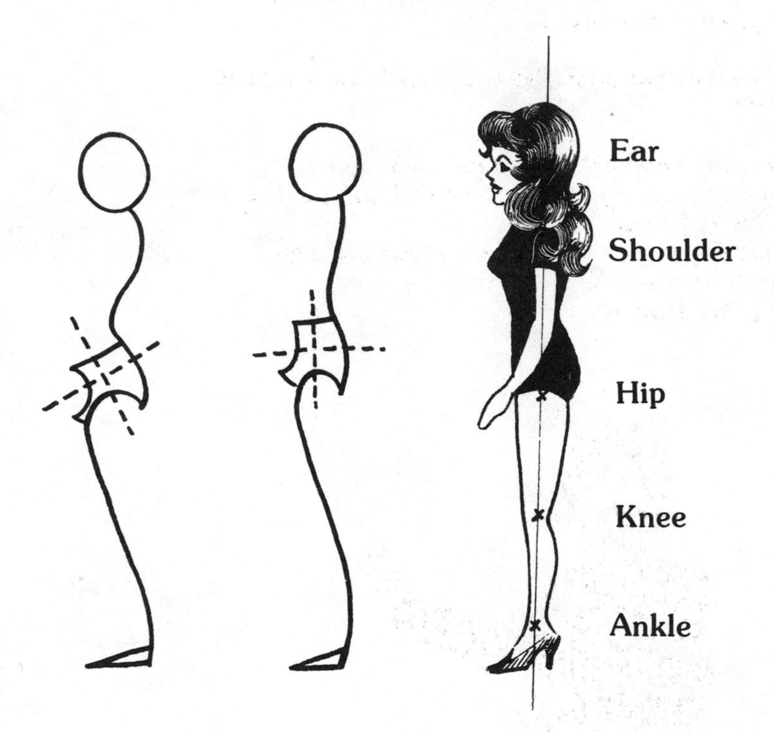

If you desire to look well on the dance floor, and develop postural habits which will serve you well in all walks of life, remember to:

Stand tall with a straight line going through the ear, shoulder, hip, knee, and ankle
Stand with the feet together and toes pointed straight ahead
Keep the hips tucked in.
Lift the diaphragm and chest and keep the head up
Carry the shoulders in a free and easy position and not forward or backward

WALKING

"Walking," as used in relation to dancing, refers to the ability of the dancer to employ the principles of correct posture as he moves gracefully about the floor in perfect time with the music. The dance walk differs only slightly for the normal walk; however, these differences are important and they should be clearly understood. When an individual learns the correct dance walk, he is well on his way to achieving success in other fundamentals of ballroom dancing. In the proper dance walk there is a curve from the back of the head to the heel of the free foot; the forward foot carries the line of posture through the ear, shoulder, hip, knee and ankle.

Following are the basic principles and procedures for mastering the dance walk:

Move the body before you move the feet
Leader, begin every step on the left foot; follower, on the right foot
Point the toes straight forward (feet parallel)
Reach from the hip
Keep the arms up

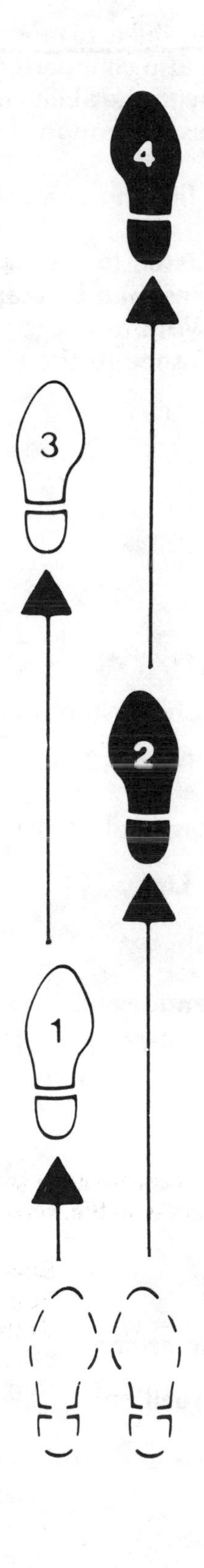

RHYTHM

The ability to move with the music is the pre-requisite for enjoyable dancing. Not only your own enjoyment, but also your partner's, depends on your ability to move in time with the music. Luckily, most people are born with the ability to move with most dance music. Everyone has a certain amount of rhythm consciousness, although it takes some longer than others to develop it.

Following is a suggested procedure for developing rhythm consciousness:

- ✓ Listen to the music
- ✓ Respond by clapping
- ✓ Walk to the rhythm
- ✓ Dance to the rhythm

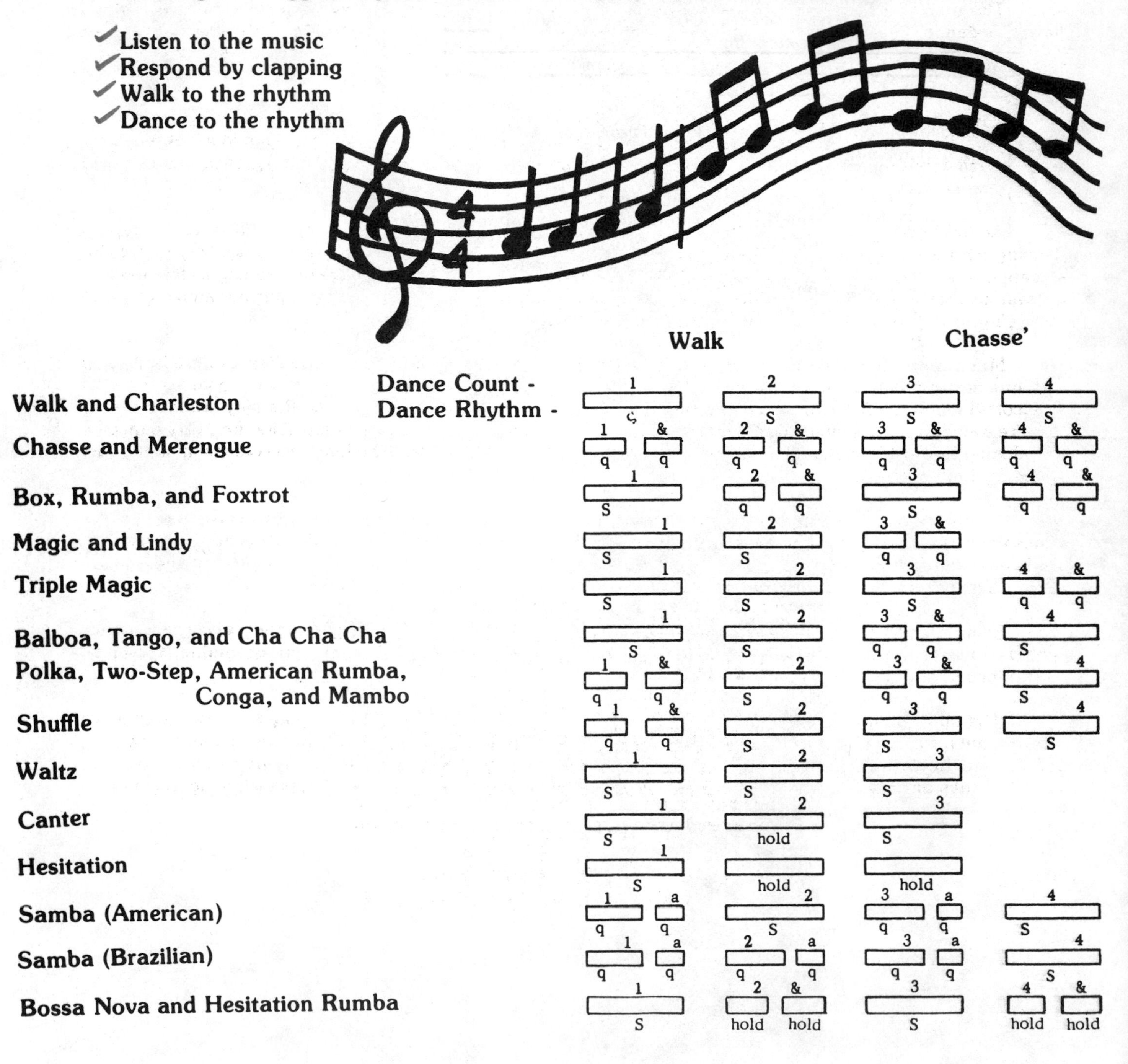

Walk — Chasse'

Dance Count - / Dance Rhythm -

	1	2	3	4
Walk and Charleston	1: S	2: S	3: S	4: S
Chasse and Merengue	1 &: q q	2 &: q q	3 &: q q	4 &: q q
Box, Rumba, and Foxtrot	1: S	2 &: q q	3: S	4 &: q q
Magic and Lindy	1: S	2: S	3 &: q q	
Triple Magic	1: S	2: S	3: S	4 &: q q
Balboa, Tango, and Cha Cha Cha	1: S	2: S	3 &: q q	4: S
Polka, Two-Step, American Rumba, Conga, and Mambo	1 &: q q	2: S	3 &: q q	4: S
Shuffle	1 &: q q	2: S	3: S	4: S
Waltz	1: S	2: S	3: S	
Canter	1: S	2: hold	3: S	
Hesitation	1: S	hold	hold	
Samba (American)	1 a: q q	2: S	3 a: q q	4: S
Samba (Brazilian)	1 a: q q	2 a: q q	3 a: q q	4: S
Bossa Nova and Hesitation Rumba	1: S	2 &: hold hold	3: S	4 &: hold hold

ETIQUETTE

For many people, the most awkward part of dancing is etiquette, but the rules of etiquette are simply guidelines for saying and doing the right thing at the right time. A great deal of the enjoyment of dancing comes from having a good time with other people, so being courteous and thoughtful is extremely important.

The man should use some finesse when asking a lady to dance. He should say something like, "May I have this dance?" He should avoid questions that require a "no"answer, such as "Is this dance taken?" or "Can you dance the samba?" "No," meaning "It isn't," or "no," meaning "Not really," might be interpreted as "No, I don't want to dance with you."

The lady should accept an invitation to dance by saying, "Certainly," "Yes, thank you," or "I'd be delighted." If she doesn't want to dance, she should politely say, "No thank you." She should never refuse an invitation to dance unless she is tired, and if she refuses an offer to dance, she should not dance the same dance with someone else.

An important part of dance etiquette is being able to converse with your partner. Whenever you begin dancing with a partner you don't know, introduce yourself and find out your partner's name. If you express sincere interest, you will have little trouble talking to each other. Admit your mistakes, apologize for stepping on your partner's toes, and so on. But don't be negative about yourself. As long as your partner knows that you are trying to improve, he or she will be very understanding.

Much of the fun of dancing comes from changing partners. A man who complains about being stuck with one partner has obviously not learned to say "Thank you." After a dance it is perfectly proper for the man to escort the lady back to her place and say, "Thank you," calling her by name. All the lady needs to say is, "You're welcome," or "I enjoyed the dance." The man sees to it that his date has a partner for every dance by introducing her to his friends and exchanging dances with other couples. The lady reserves the first and last dance for her escort.

Another important part of etiquette is making proper introductions. When acquaintances meet on the dance floor, the individuals who know each other should introduce their partners to the other couple. If you do not hear a name, it is proper to ask that it be repeated. If there is any doubt about whether individuals know each other, the person making the introductions should ask a question to that effect.

Keep in mind the nature of the occasion. Dress appropriately and remember unnecessary necessaries such as flowers. Because the way you look is just as important as the way you act, your grooming, as well as your dancing, should reflect your best efforts.

The man should always treat the woman like a lady--opening doors for her, taking her coat, getting her refreshments, holding her chair, helping her through a crowd, and so forth. Even if a man's dance partner is not his date, he should be so polite as to escort her to and from the dance floor. By the same token, the woman should always act like a lady and allow, not force, her partner to be a gentleman. Expressing appreciation - for the man's courtesy will work wonders.

POSITIONS

The key to freedom of movement in dancing is using the correct position, enabling the man to give effective leads and allows both partners to execute each step in the most efficient manner.

Closed Position

The man and the lady stand directly in front of each other with their toes pointing straight forward and almost touching. The man's right hand is on the small of the lady's back, and the fingertips of the lady's left hand rest lightly on the top of the man's right shoulder. The man's left arm is extended straight out to his side, with the elbow bent and the wrist straight, so that his hand is at the height of the woman's chin. The man's and lady's shoulders are parallel, and each dancer's head is turned slightly to the left, looking over the partner's shoulder.

Conversation Position

Conversation position. The basic position for sideward steps. It is almost identical to closed position except that the partners stand slightly farther apart to have greater freedom of movement.

Semi-Open Position

Reverse Position

Open Position

Right-Side Position

Roll Position

Two-Hand Position

Back To Back Position

Shine (Individual or Challenge) Position

Left-Side Position

Varsouvienne or
Sweetheart Position

FOOT MOVEMENTS

The feet may be moved in one of eight basic directions. The figure on the left illustrates these directions for the lady's right foot. The figure on the right illustrates the basic directions for the gentleman's left foot.

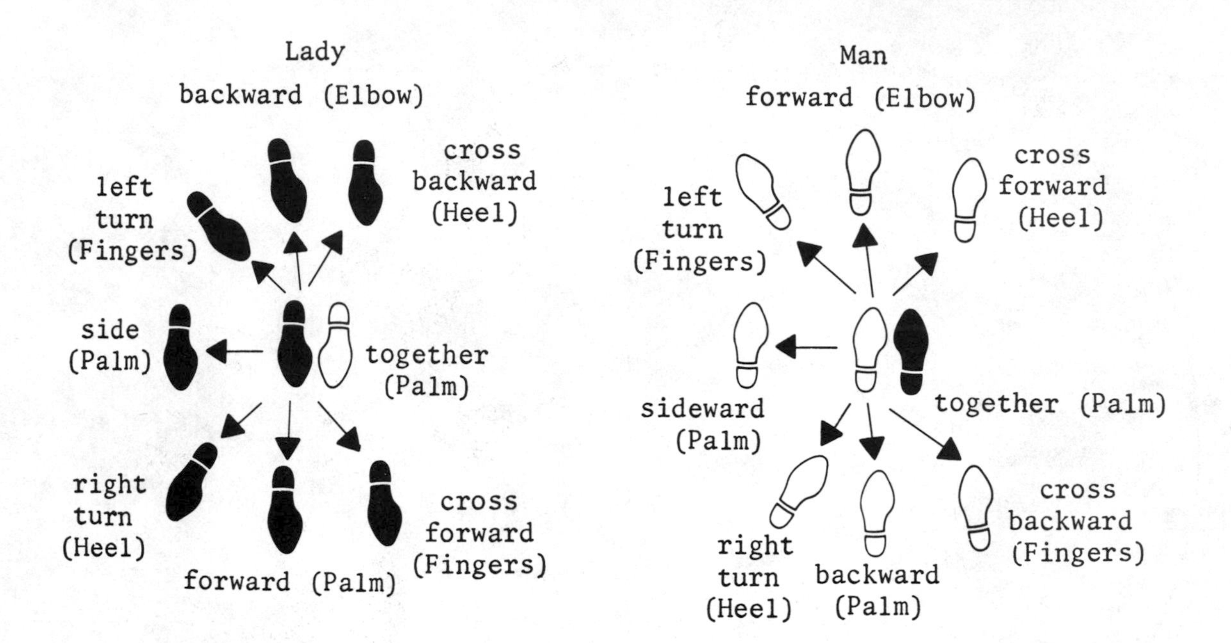

The eight basic directions for the lady when she begins on the right foot and the lead for each direction is as follows (when the leader raises his elbow, lady steps backward):

Direction	Lead
Backward	Elbow
Backward cross	Heel, leverage F
Left turn	Fingers
Forward	Palm
Forward cross	Fingers, leverage B
Right turn	Heel
Side	Palm
Together	Palm

The eight basic directions for the man when he begins on the left foot, and the lead for each are as follows:

Foot Movement	Hand Lead	Body Lead	Directions
Forward	Elbow	Leverage	Forward
Left turn	Fingers	Leverage	Forward
Sideward left	Palm	Leverage	Left
Backward	Palm	Leverage	Backward
Right turn	Heel	Leverage	Backward
Cross forward	Heel	Leverage	Forward
Cross backward	Fingers	Leverage	Backward

LINE OF DANCE

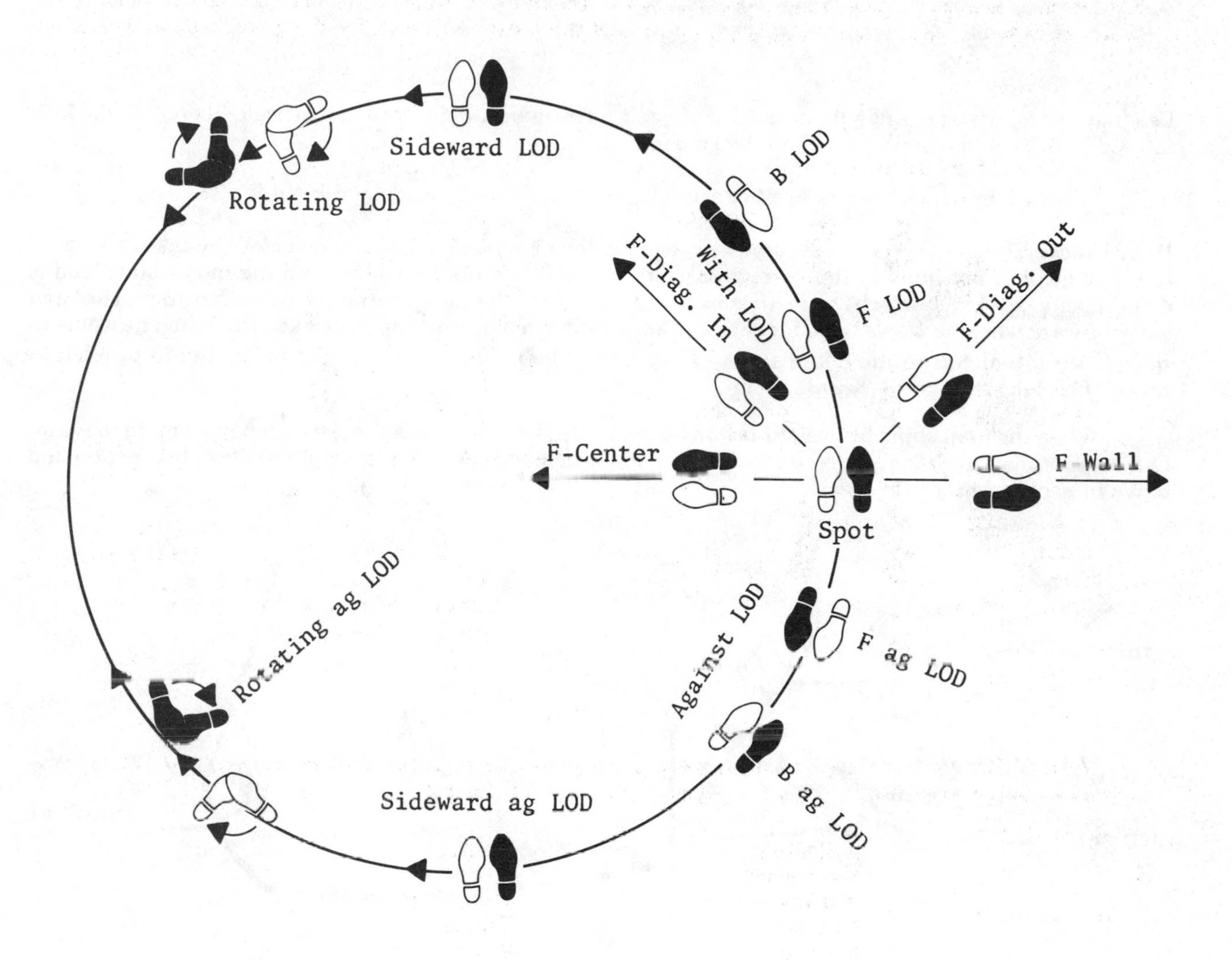

Dancers may travel forward, backward, sideward, or rotate in any line of dance

LEADING

Leading and following are like the two sides of a coin. The man should learn to lead well, but unless the lady follows well, their movements will not be smooth.

In ballroom dancing there are two basic types of leads--body leads and hand leads.

Body Leads. The man gives a body lead by leaning in the direction he wants to go before he takes a step. If the lady has her left hand in the correct position on the man's right shoulder and the man's body lead is definite, she will know which way she is expected to move before her partner steps on her toe. The man leans forward when he wants to go forward and backward when he wants to go backward. When he wants to go sideward, he leans to the left or right. To turn right he moves right shoulder back, and to turn left he moves his right shoulder forward.

When the man shifts his weight before taking a step, he creates leverage, which helps him to move into a step. When he changes directions, he must counterbalance or shift his weight to offset his motion and move in another direction.

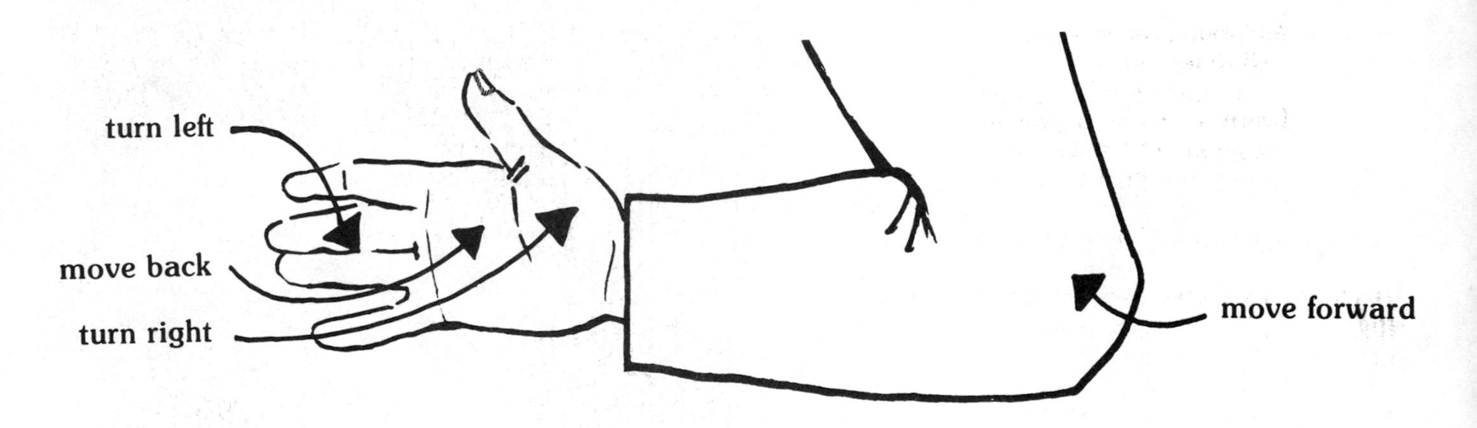

Hand Leads. Sometimes the lady may interpret a body lead in several ways. For example, when the man moves his right shoulder forward, he may intend that she turn left or change positions. Consequntly, the body lead must always be accompanied by a hand lead. The body lead indicates the direction the lady should move, and the hand lead indicates the position she should take.

If the man's right hand is placed correctly on the small of the lady's back, he can maneuver his partner with very slight hand movements. If the partners are in closed position and the man wants to move forward, he raises his right elbow without raising his shoulder, slightly lifting his partner's left arm. If he wants to move backward, he presses lightly against his partner's back with the palm of his right hand. If he wants to move sideward left or right, he maintains normal pressure with the palm of his right hand and indicates the direction he wishes to go with a body lead. When the man wants to turn right, he gives more pressure with the heel of his right hand, and when he wants to turn left, he gives more pressure with the fingers of his right hand. The man should always maintain the body lead and hand lead until he changes directions or positions.

FOLLOWING

"Following" refers to the ability of the lady to respond quickly, easily, and correctly to any indication of change in position, direction, rhythm, or step given by her partner.

A good follower observes the following

- Know the basic ballroom dance steps.
- Maintain proper position at all times.
- Learn the leads for the basic positons and steps:

    1. Raised elbow--follower moves backward.
    2. Palm-follower moves forward, sideward, or makes no change.
    3. Heel of the right hand--follower turns right.
    4. Fingers of the right hand--follower turns left
    5. Right shoulder forward--follower turns left when in closed position.
    6. Right shoulder backward--follower turns right when in closed position.

- Follow the path of least resistance.
- Support your own weight.
- Do not attempt to lead your partner.
- Keep the left hand on the top of the leader's right shoulder.
- Maintain proper balance at all times.

PART II

EIGHT BASICS

There are four possible combinations of foot movements and weight changes. A foot movement accompanied by a weight change is called a step. In a walk step the free foot extends out from the supporting foot and receives the weight. In a chasse' step (pronounced "shaw-say"") the free foot comes together or closes with the supporting foot and receives the weight. A foot movement without a weight change is called a hesitation. A dancer may hesitate by touching his toe to the floor, drawing his free foot toward his supporting foot, or kicking with his free foot. He may also brush the floor with his free foot, point it, lift it, swing it, or dot his free foot behind his supporting foot. A change is a weight change without a foot movement, and a hold has neither a foot movement nor a weight change.

When possible foot movements and weight changes are combined with possible music rhythms and dance rhythms, the result is hundreds of possible dance steps.

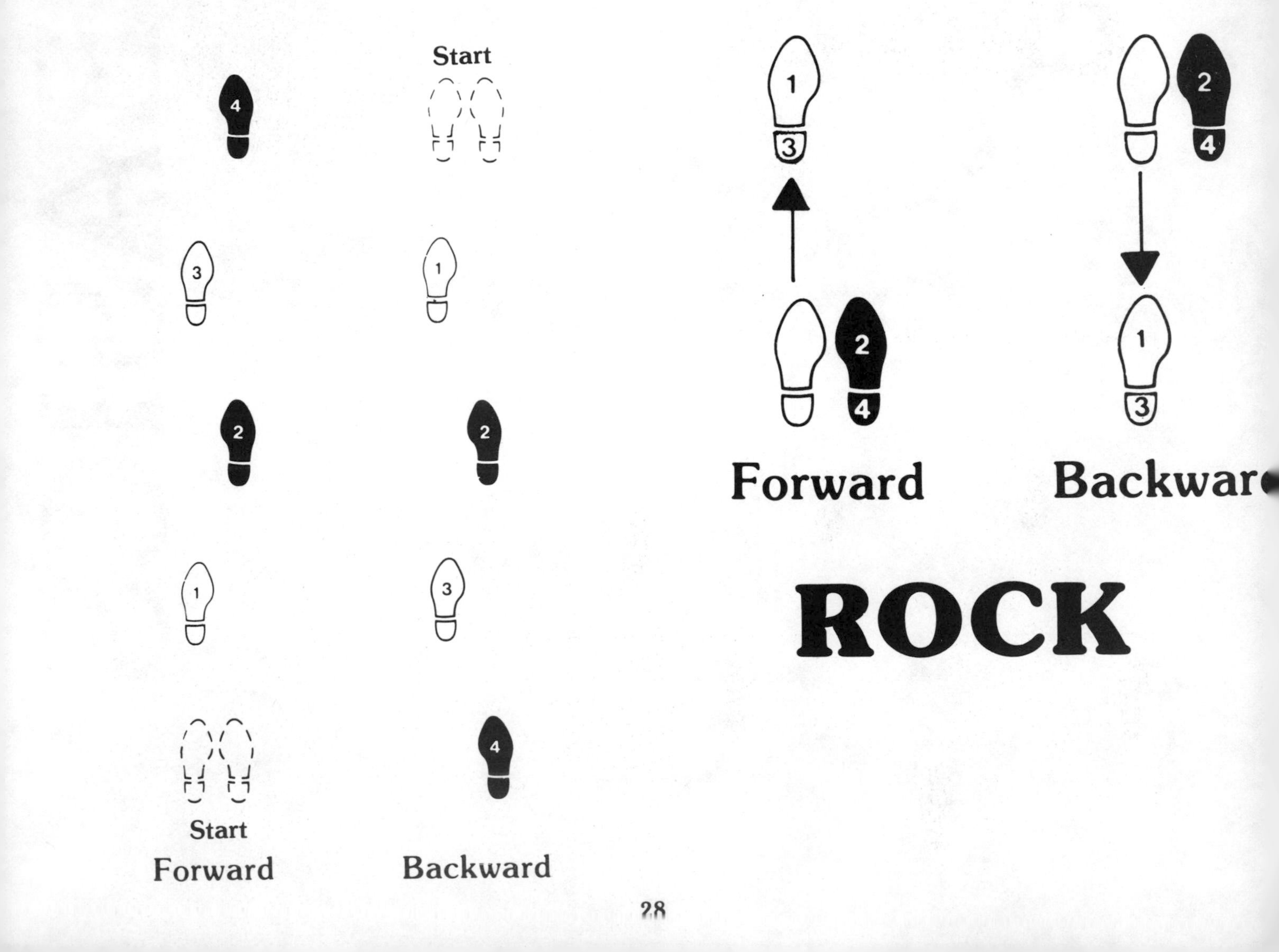

Junior Cross
(Lady dances same as man)

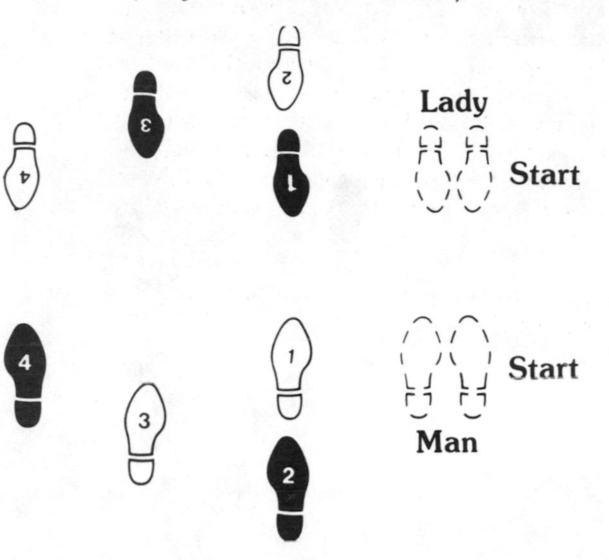

Senior Cross
(Lady dances opposite man)

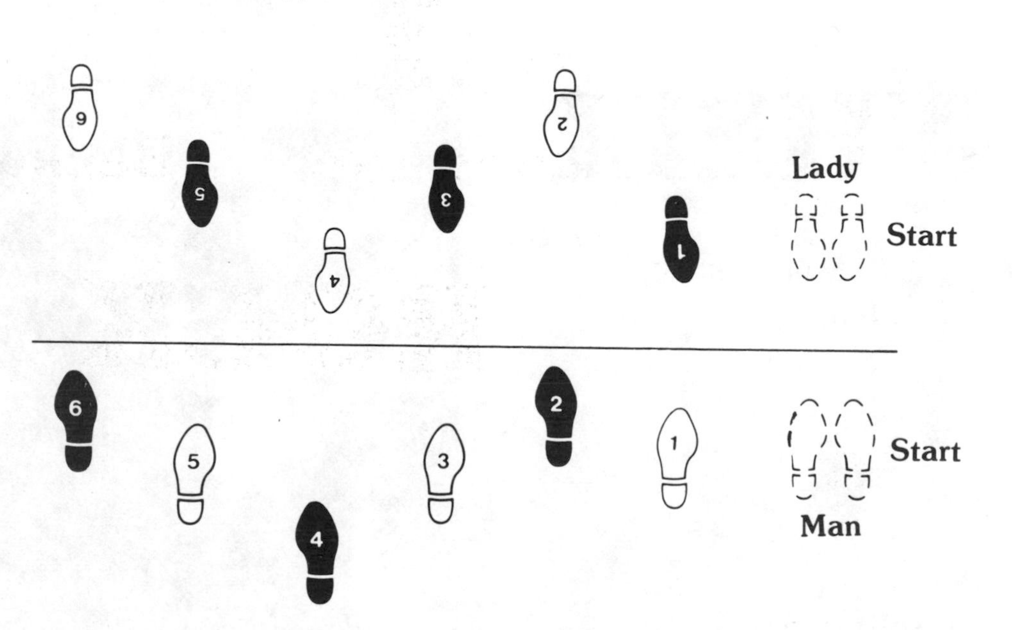

ARCH

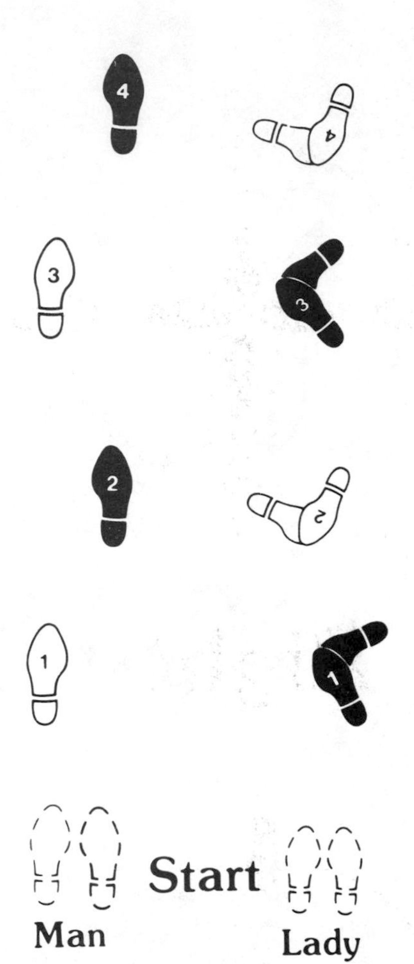

WHEEL

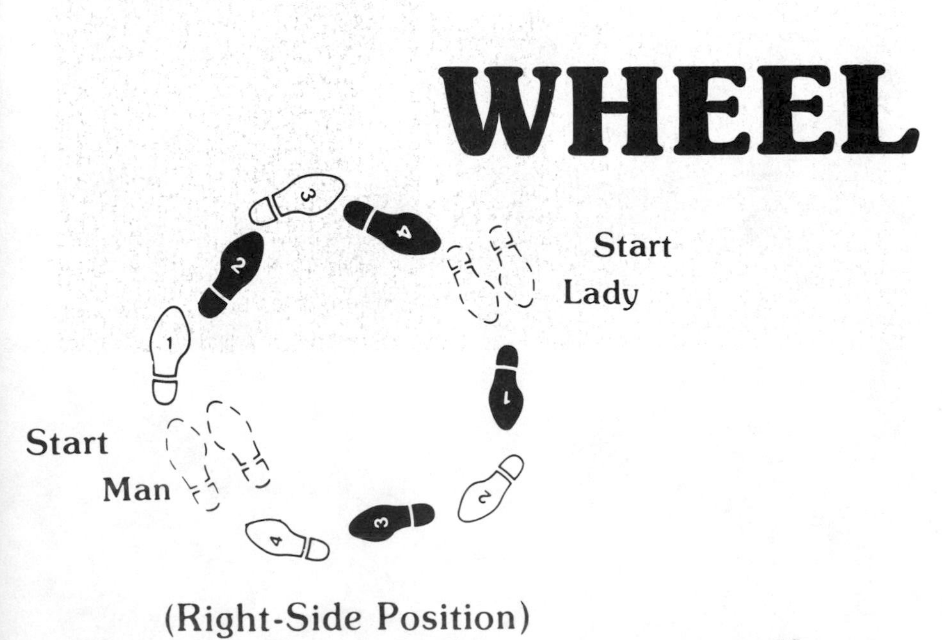

(Right-Side Position)

PIVOT

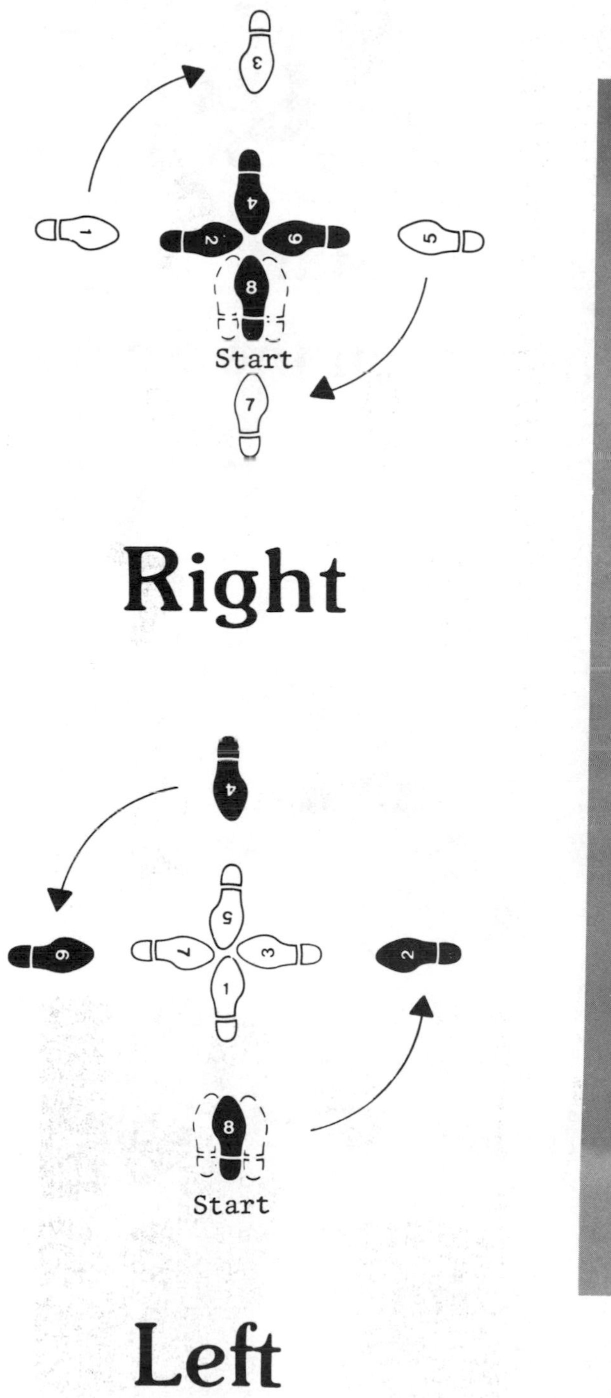
Start
Right
Start
Left

CHASSE'

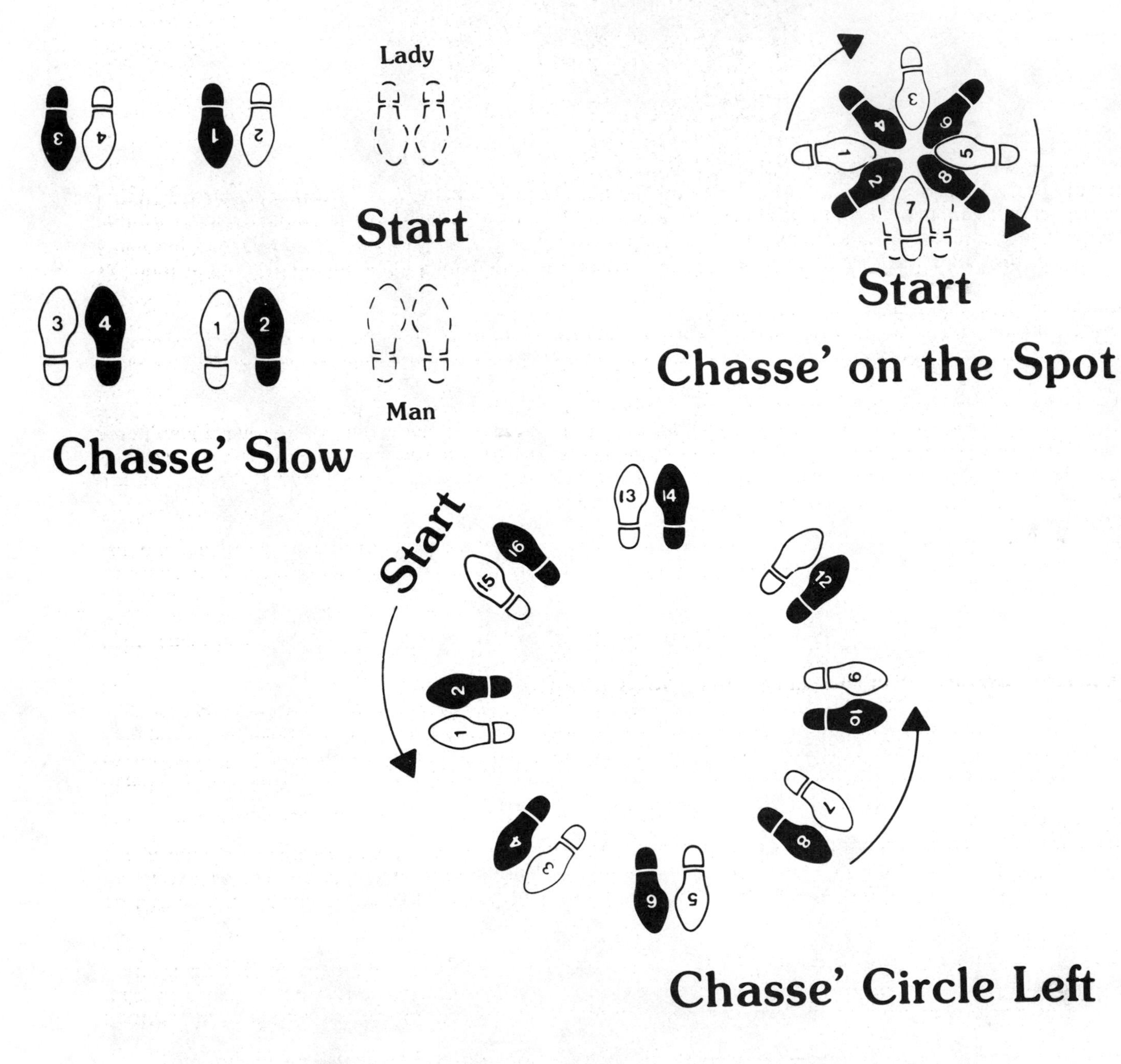

Chasse' Slow

Chasse' on the Spot

Chasse' Circle Left

Start

Chasse' Rhythm

HESITATION

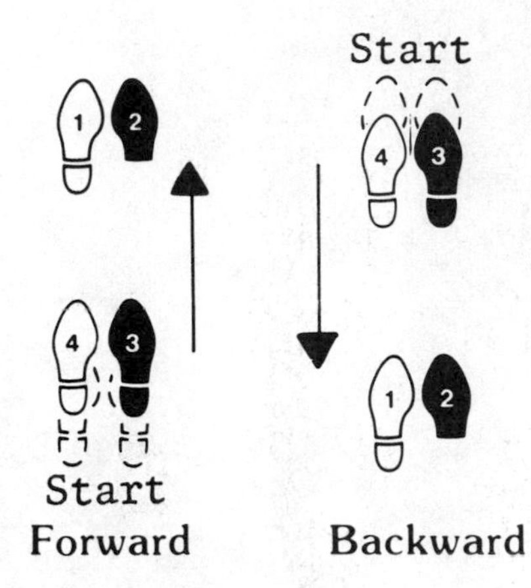

Sideward

Progressive Forward Basic

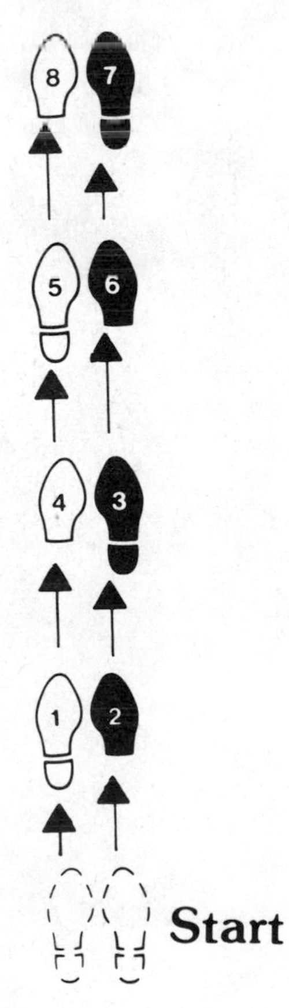

PART III

AMERICAN DANCE

FOXTROT

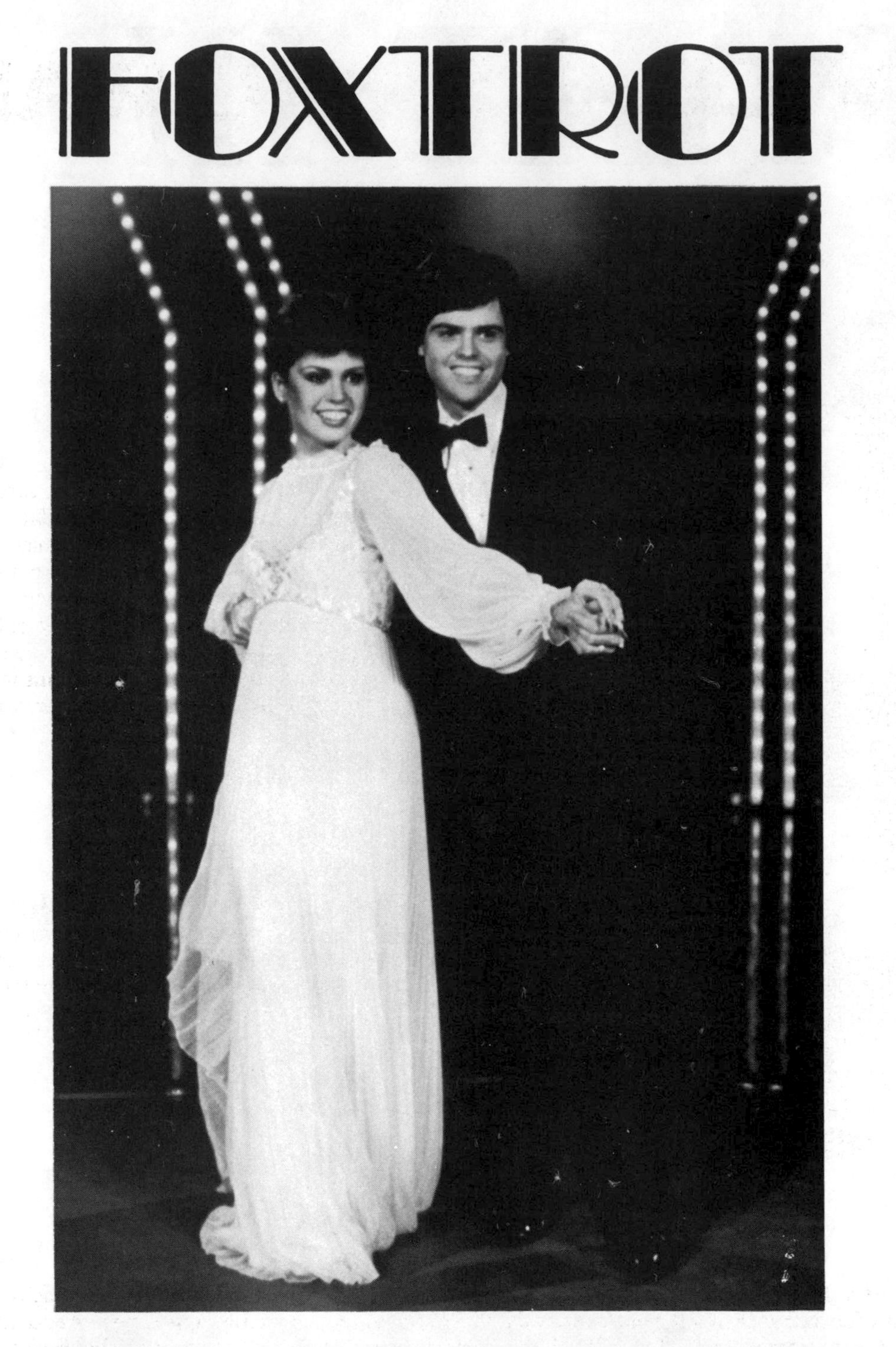

The foxtrot was named after Harry Fox, a musical comedy star who introduced the basic step in Florenz Ziegfeld's show during the 1913-14 season. The dance, a trotting step done to the then popular ragtime, was a show-stopper. Its popularity was given a tremendous boost when it was readily adapted to popular blues rhythms.

Oscar Duryea, a contemporary dancing teacher, was asked to use Harry Fox's routine in a ballroom demonstration for a group in a New York hotel. He combined the two-step, Harry Fox's running steps, and slow walking steps. From this beginning the foxtrot has spread to a great variety of steps. By the early twenties the foxtrot had emerged as the basic dance form in America.

Over the years the foxtrot has been so streamlined that most of the trotting has been eliminated, and it has become smooth and graceful. Today the foxtrot, the only smooth ballroom dance that originated in America, is danced all over the world.

DANCE #1 BASIC WALK

The basic walk step is the easiest step in dancing. The difference between walking and doing the basic walk step is merely maintaining correct walking posture. A unit of walk rhythm consists of two optional steps, which may be forward, backward, or sideward. Since each unit takes only two beats of music, a measure of walk rhythm contains two units. The man begins every unit with his left foot, and the lady begins every unit with her right foot.

TEMPO--There is a wide range of foxtrot tempos, varying from very slow to very fast. Quick steps are used frequently in slow tempos while slow tempos slow steps seem to fit fast tempos best; that is, as the tempo increases, more slow and fewer quick steps are used.

A forward walk unit is made up of two forward steps, and a backward walk unit is made up of two backward steps. In both the forward walk and the backward walk the free foot moves past the supporting foot and takes the weight, thus becoming the supporting foot. As the free foot passes the supporting foot, it ceases to be the following foot and becomes the leading foot. A forward rock unit is composed of a forward movement and a backward movement, and a backward rock unit is composed of a backward movement, then a forward movement. In both the forward rock and the backward rock the free foot remains in place and the weight is shifted back to it.

The forward walk, backward walk, forward rock, and backward rock are all done in closed position, which means that the lady's footwork is the opposite of the man's. In other words, when the man steps forward, the lady steps backward, and vice versa.

In the step description column capital letters indicate slow movements and lower case letters indicate quick movements. Underlined letters when used in connection with parenthesis indicates when action within parenthesis takes place.

Basic Forward	Closed	F F F F	Elbow
Basic Backward	Closed	B B B B	Palm
Mark Time	Closed	L R L R - L R L R (in place)	Palm

Forward Walk

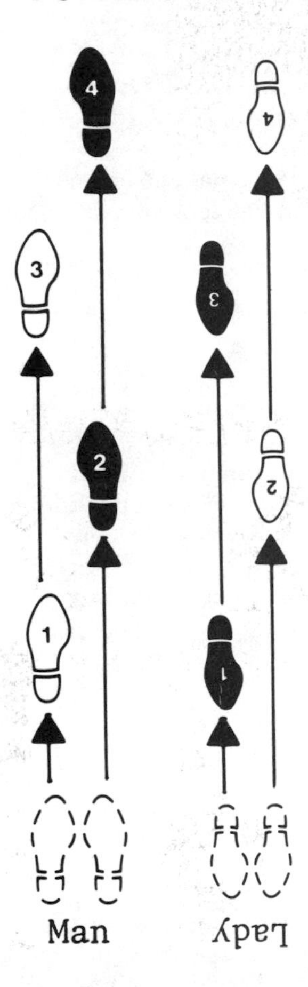

Backward Walk

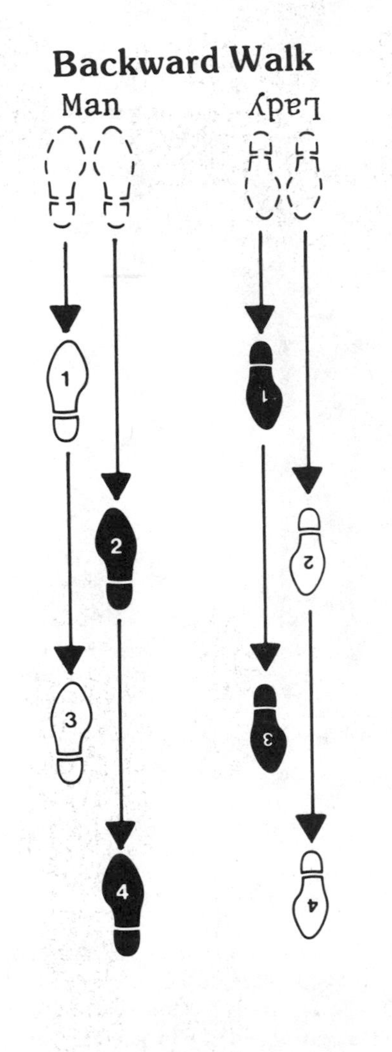

Junior Walk	Semi-open Reverse	F F F F (TR ½ to Rev P) B B B B (TL ½ to S O P) G F F F F (TL ½ to Rev P) B B B B (TR ½ to S O P)	Palm Fingers Heel
Senior Walk	R & L Side	F F F F (TR ½ to L Sd P) B B B B (TL ½ to R Sd P)	Elbow Heel, Palm Fingers

Junior Walk

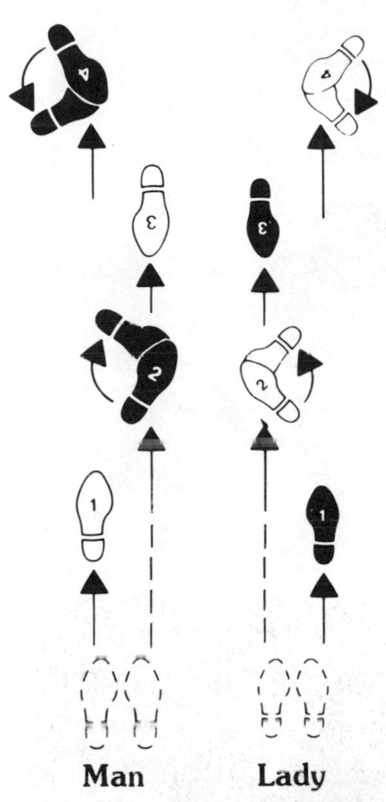

Senior Walk

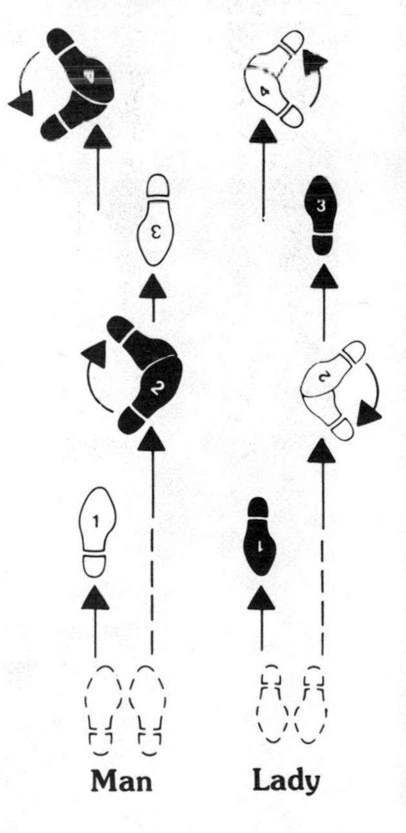

Rock steps consist of moving back and forth or sideward, without moving the feet but with a change of weight. Rock steps can be used in any dance or can be combined with any other step. They ususally are danced on the spot, but can be used for progressing or traveling around the dance floor when combined with other steps.

In the sideward rock the weight is shifted from side to side. The man creates leftward leverage and shifts his weight to the left, then counterbalances right and shifts his weight back to the right. Meanwhile he maintains normal pressure on his partner's back with the palm of his right hand. The body leads and hand leads are repeated on beats 3 and 4.

In the forward walk and the backward walk the free foot passes the supporting foot in the "left foot lane" or "right foot lane." However, in a sideward walk the free foot must go in front of or behind the supporting foot. Consequently, there are two lanes of traffic moving sideward--a front lane and a back lane.

ROCK STEPS

Sideward Rock

Lady

1 3 2 4

Man

1 3 2 4

Forward Rock

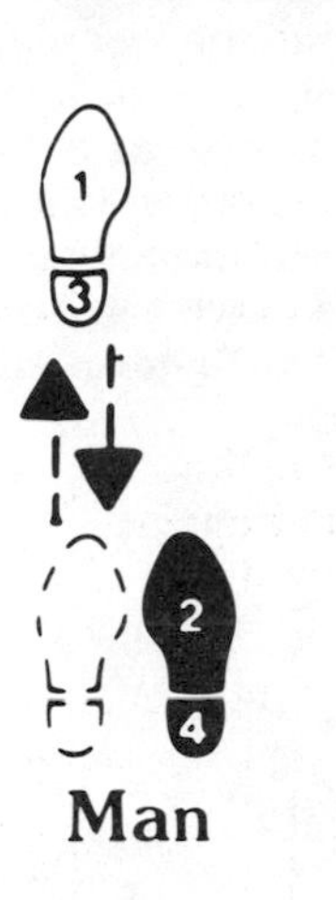

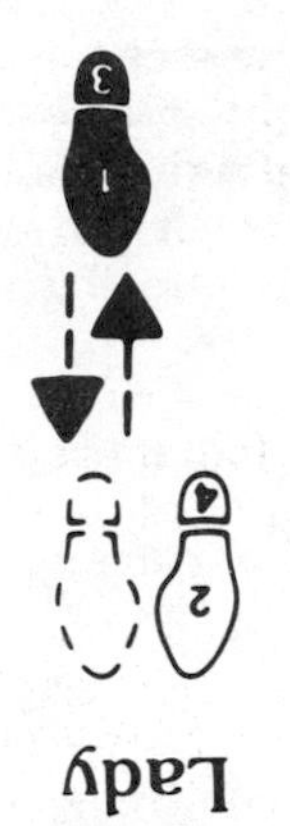

Backward Rock

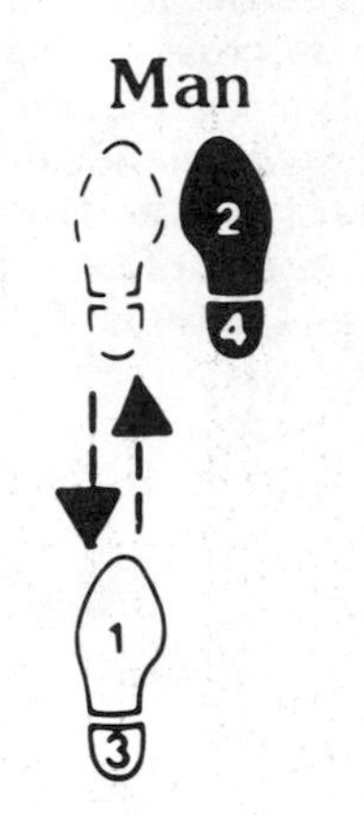

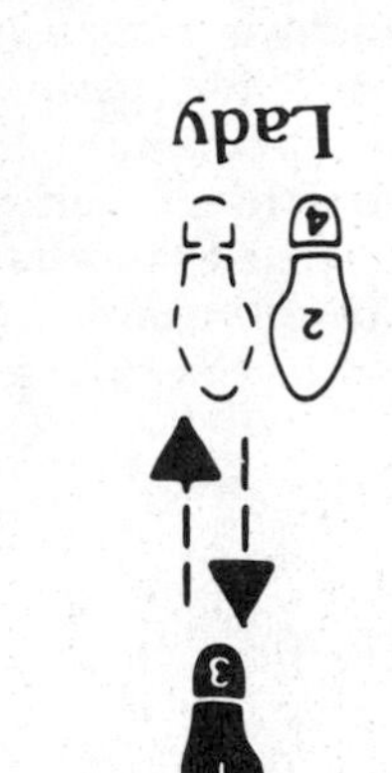

Step	Position	Directions	Hand Lead
Forward Rock	Closed	F B F B	Elbow, Palm
Left Rock Turn	Closed	F B F B-F B F B (TL 1) 	Fingers
Backward Rock	Closed	B F B F	Palm, Elbow
Right Rock Turn	Closed	B F B F-B F B F (TR 1)	Heel

Right Rock Turn

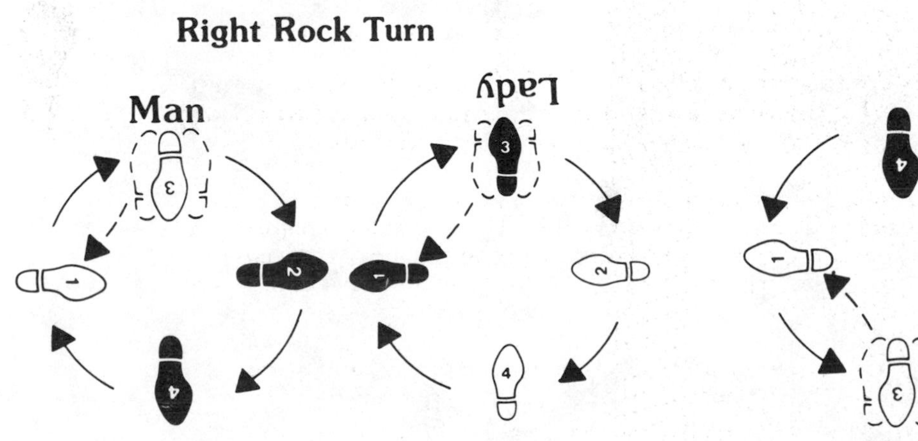

Left Rock Turn

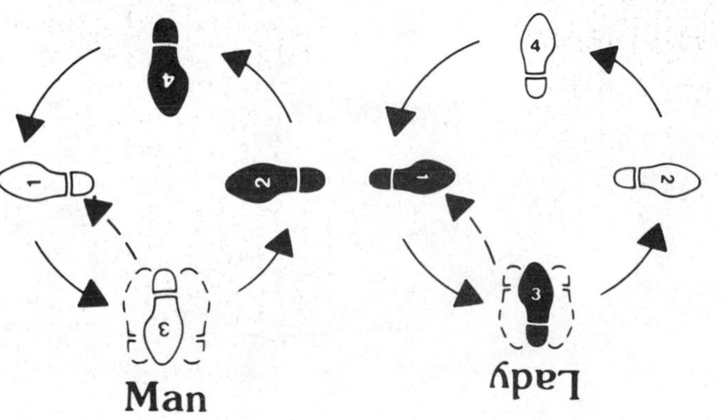

Cross steps generaly are danced to the side, in any position or rhythm. They can be combined with any other step. Care should be taken to keep the shoulders parallel. If the body is turned too far with cross steps, the steps become forward or backward steps. Cross steps are made by crossing the free foot either in front of or behind the supporting foot. When partners cross their feet both forward and back at the same time, in the same direction, requiring a semi-open and reverse position, the step is referred to as a Junior-Cross. If they cross opposite to one another, requiring a left-side and a right-side position, the step is referred to as a Senior Cross. Cross steps are led with the fingers and heel of the right hand, accompanied with a body lead. For example: (1) to get the girl to cross her right foot behind her left foot, lead with the heel and lean to the right; (2) to get the girl to cross her right foot in front of the left foot, lead with the fingers and lean to the right.

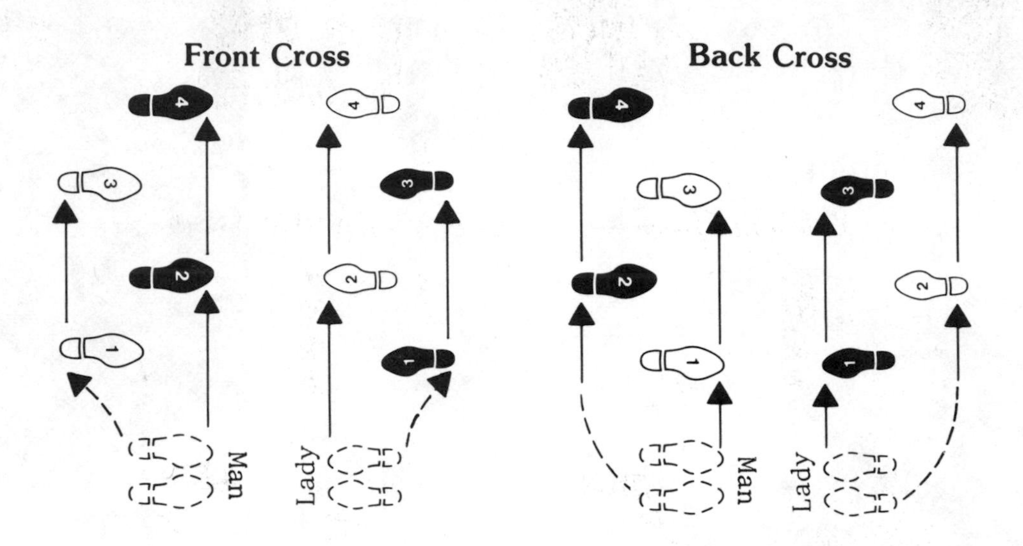

Step	Position	Directions	Hand Lead
Front Cross	Conversation	Bk Fr Bk Fr Left	Heel
Back Cross	Conversation	Fr Bk Fr Bk Left	Fingers
Front/Back Cross	Conversation	Bk Fr Fr Bk Left	Heel, Fingers

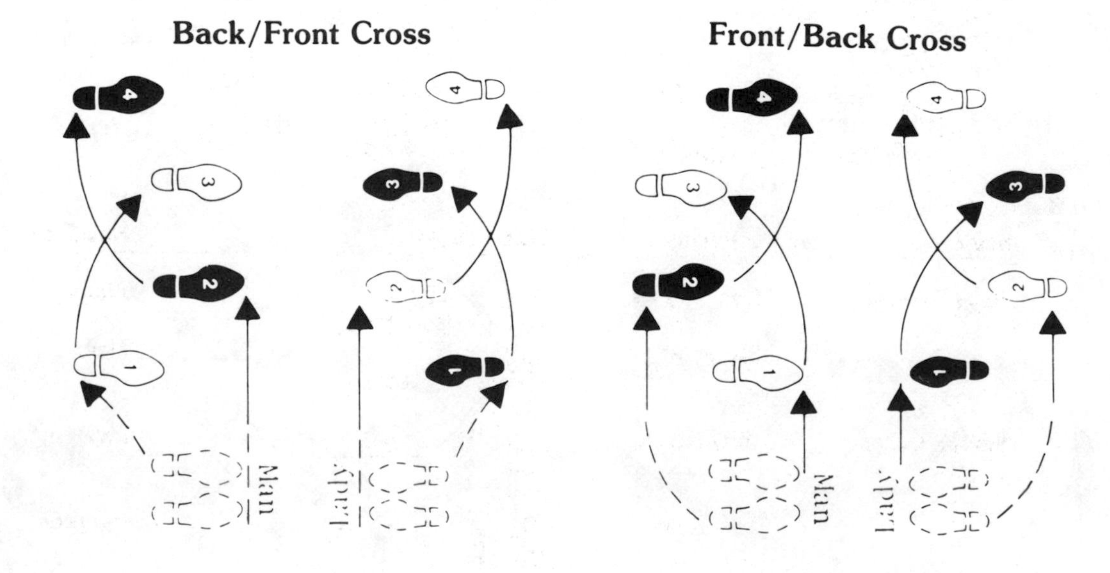

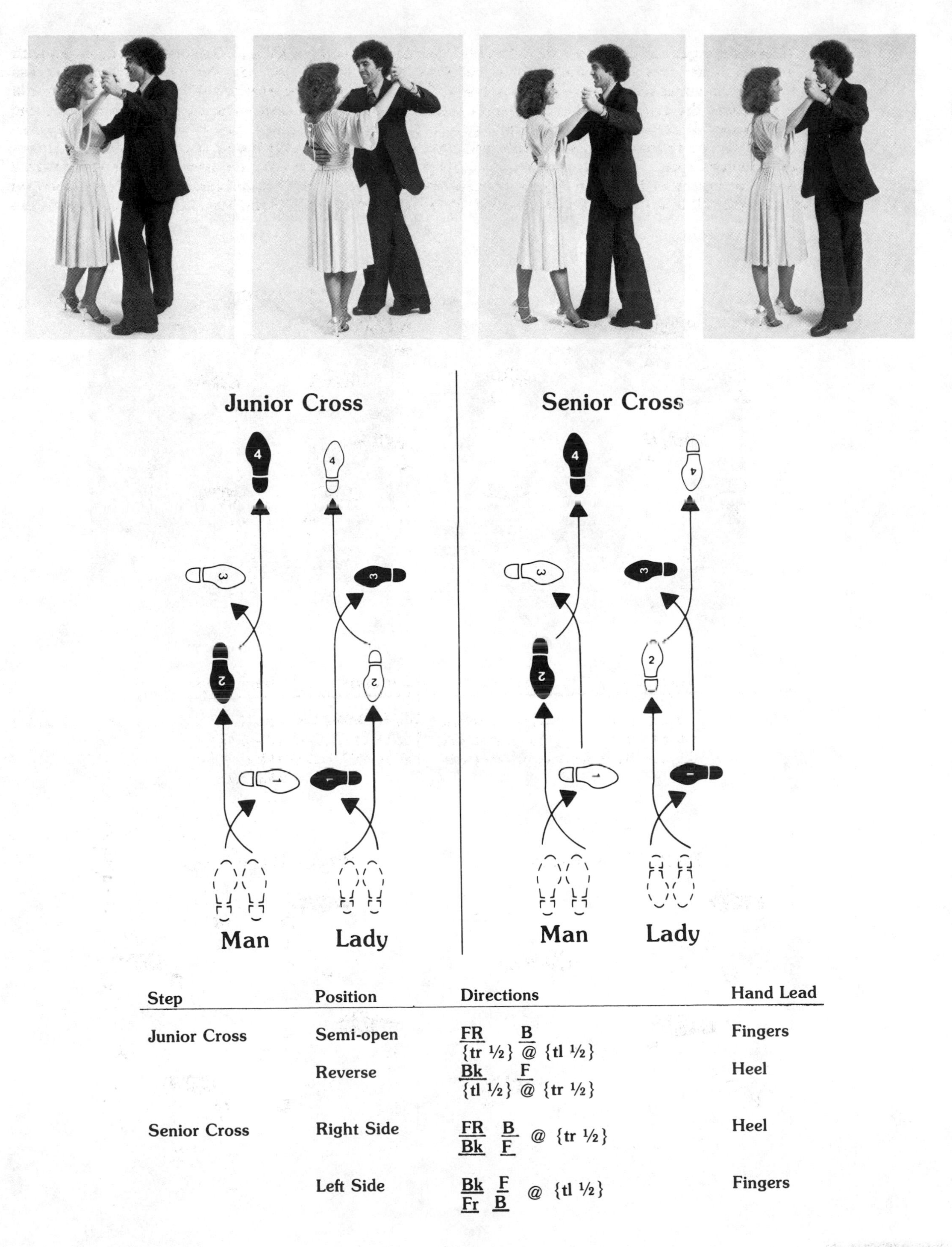

Step	Position	Directions	Hand Lead
Junior Cross	Semi-open	FR / {tr ½} B / @ {tl ½}	Fingers
	Reverse	Bk / {tl ½} F / @ {tr ½}	Heel
Senior Cross	Right Side	FR / Bk B / F @ {tr ½}	Heel
	Left Side	Bk / Fr F / B @ {tl ½}	Fingers

Forward Arch Backward Arch

For the arch steps partners join one hand and raise them high enough for one or both dancers to go under the raised arms. Four contacts are possible; right right, left left, right left, and left right. The girl always goes under the arch unless otherwise indicated.

arches may be danced with any other step or position, but the arch itself is danced in open, two-hand, or crossed hands position.

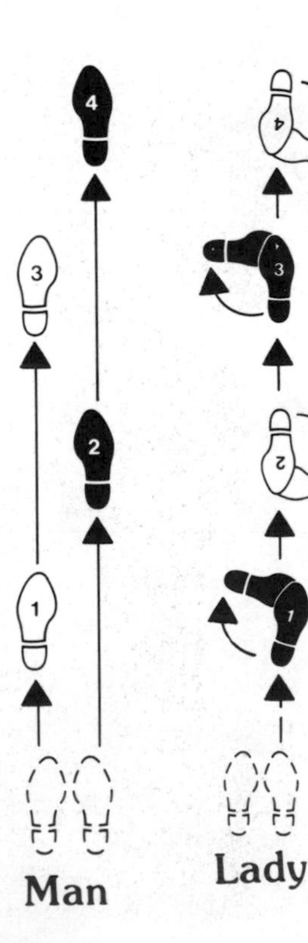

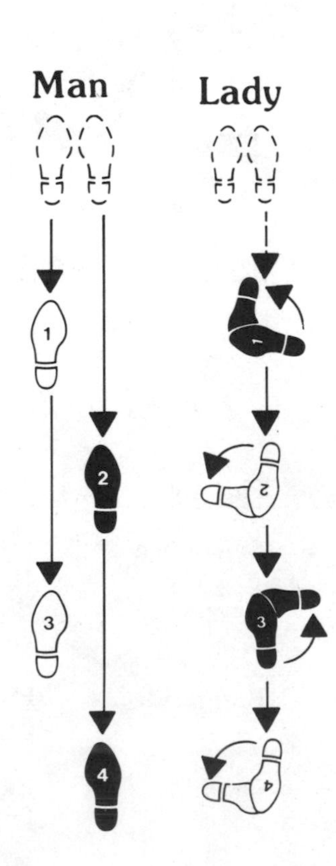

WHEELS

Wheel steps are danced turning around an imaginary pivot point in positions other than closed, conversation, or shine. Dancers may be turning: (a) both forward--right or left side, right hand or left hand; (b) both backward--right or left side.

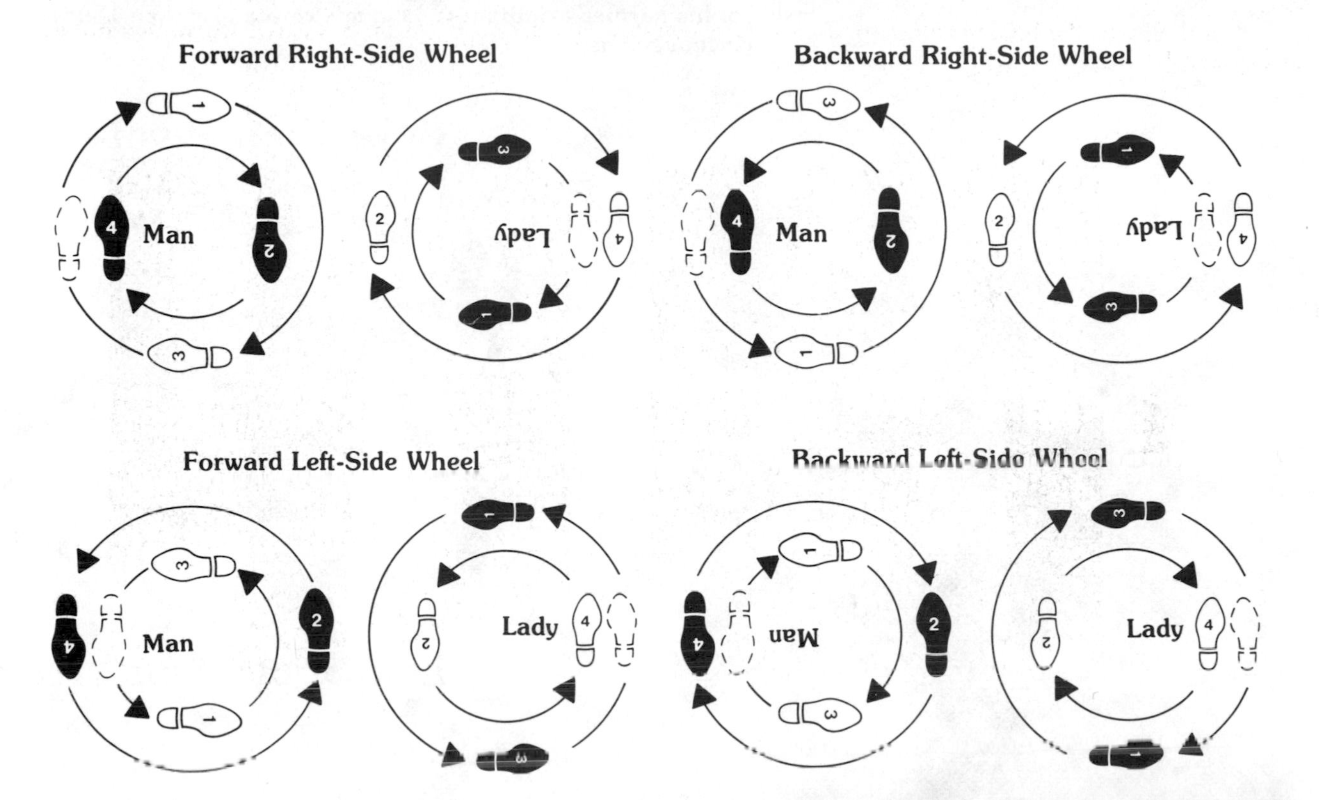

Step	Position	Step Description	Hand Lead
Forward R Sd Wheel	R Side	F F F F (TR 1) G Same	Palm Heel
Forward L Sd Wheel	L Side	F F F F (TL 1) G Same	Palm Fingers
Backward R Sd Wheel	R Side	B B B B (TL 1) G Same	Elbow Fingers
Backward L Sd Wheel	L Side	B B B B (TR 1) G Same	Left Hand Heel of R H

PIVOT STEPS

In the place pivot the partners rotate around a stationary pivot point which is the man's right foot forward and against the inside of his partner's right foot. Dancers rotate less than 180° on each movement.

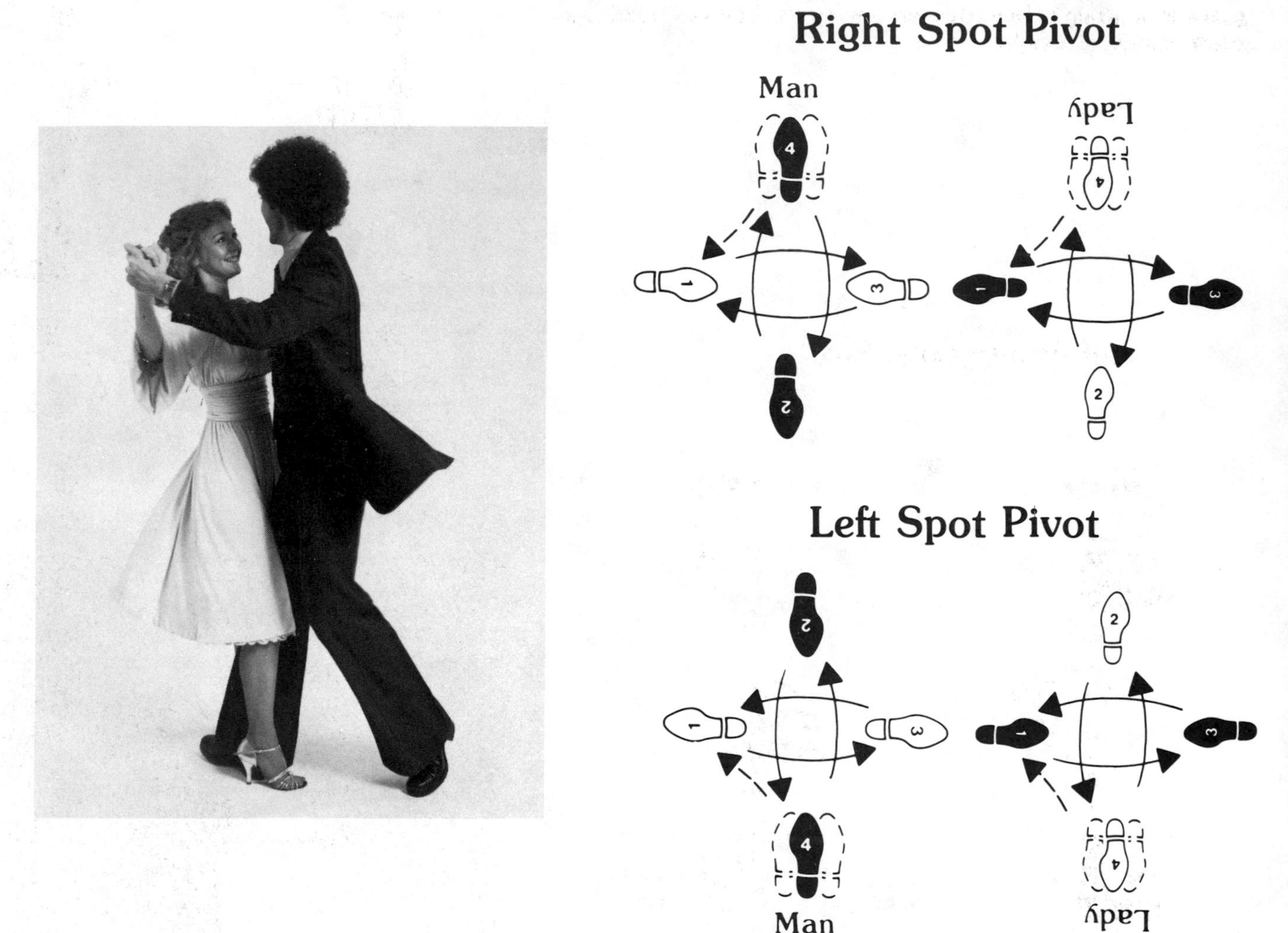

Name of Step	Position	Directional Call And Step Description	Man's Hand Leads
In Place Pivot Right	Closed	B F B F (Pv R 2)	Heel Palm
Progressive Pivot Right	Closed	B F B F (Pv R 2)	Heel Palm
Pivot Left in Place	Closed	F B F B (Pv L 1)	Fingers Palm
Progressive Left Pivot	Closed	F B F B (TL 2)	Fingers Palm

Right Progressive Pivot

In the progressive pivot the dancers rotate around a moving pivot point as they move in line of direction around the hall on each step. Most dancers have difficulty traveling in a straight line while doing the progressive pivot, and consequently move in a large counterclockwise circle as they pivot. In order to progress in a straight line, dancers must turn half way (180°) on each change of weight.

Left Progressive Pivot

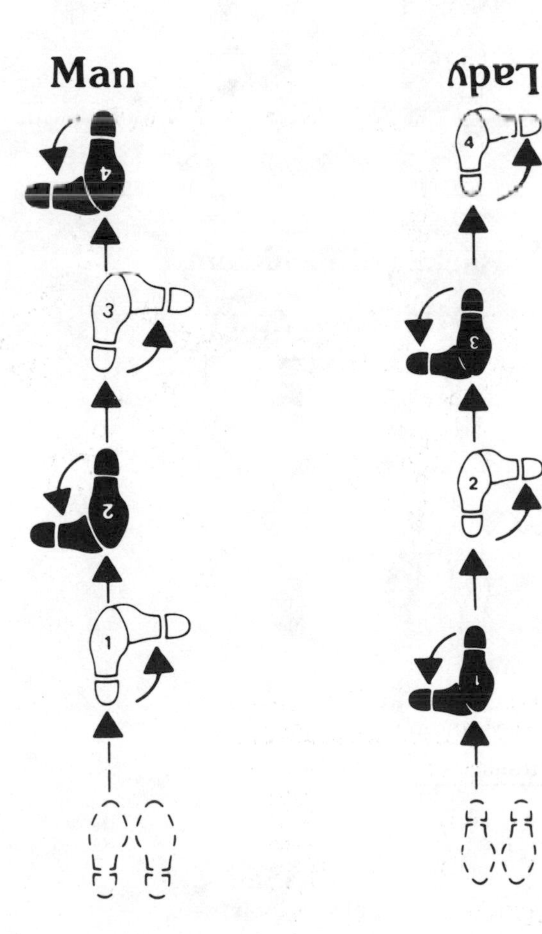

CHASSE' STEPS

A unit of chasse' rhythm consists of an optional step and a mandatory step. The man begins each unit by stepping forward, backward, or sideward with his left foot, then closes with his right foot, bringing his feet together on every second step. The lady begins each unit with her right foot and closes with her left. Because the following foot never passes the leading foot, this rhythm is appropriately called the chasse' or "chase."

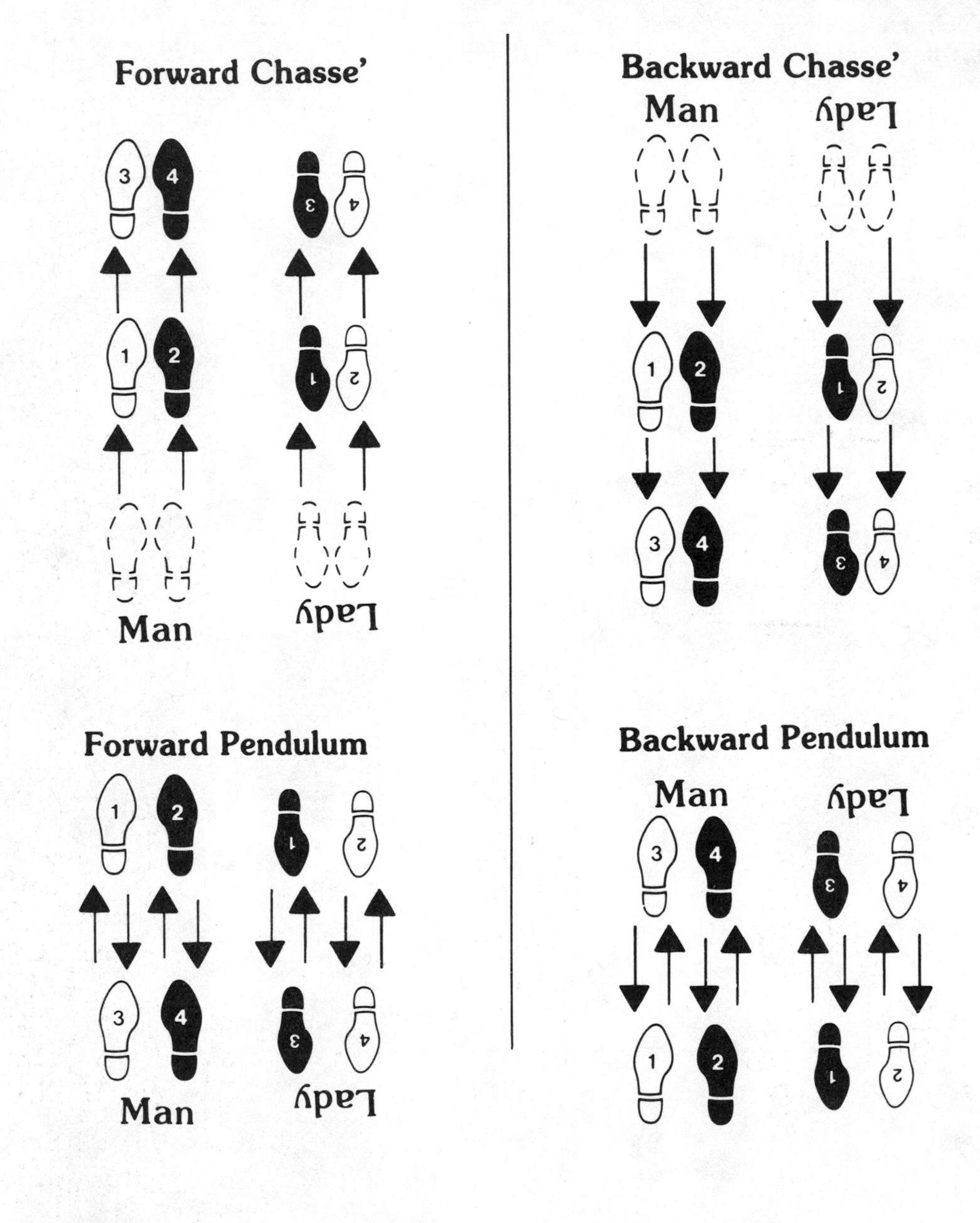

Step	Position	Directions	Hand Lead
Forward Chasse'	Closed	f cl f cl	Elbow
Backward Chasse'	Closed	b cl b cl	Palm
Forward Pendulum	Closed	f cl b cl	Elbow, Palm
Backward Pendulum	Closed	b cl f cl	Palm, Elbow

In the sideward chasse' the man gives a palm lead, then steps to the side with his left foot and closes with his right. The lady steps to the side with her right foot and closes with her left.

Step	Position	Directions	Body Lead	Hand Lead
Sideward Chasse'	Conversation	sd cl sd cl	Left	Palm

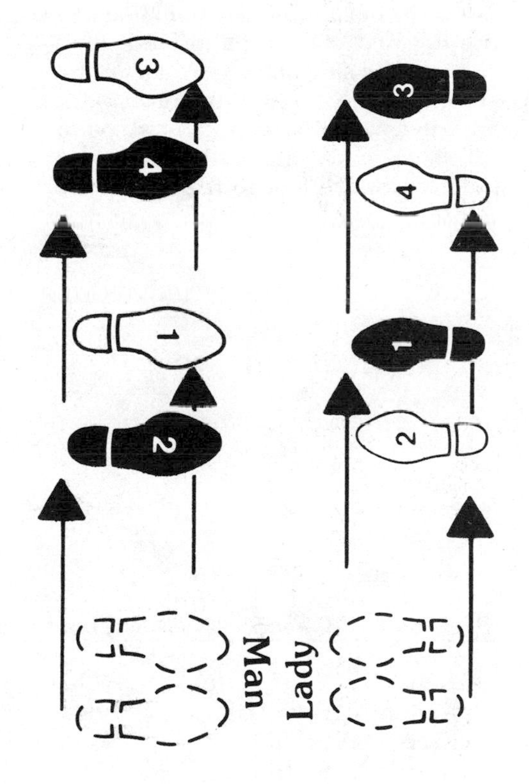

HESITATION

Each unit of hesitation rhythm consists of an optional forward, backward, or sideward step and a mandatory hesitation. The only difference between the step pattern of the hesitation rhythm and those of the chasse' rhythm is that in the hesitation the free foot touches to the side of the supporting foot rather than receiving the weight because each unit involves only one weight change, a measure of hesitation rhythm consists of two units. The man begins the first unit on his left foot and the second unit on his right; the lady begins the first unit on her right foot and the second unit on her left.

In both the dance rhthym and the step directions and hesitation is indicated by parenthesis. Each foot movement required one full beat, regardless of weight changes.

Sideward Hesitation

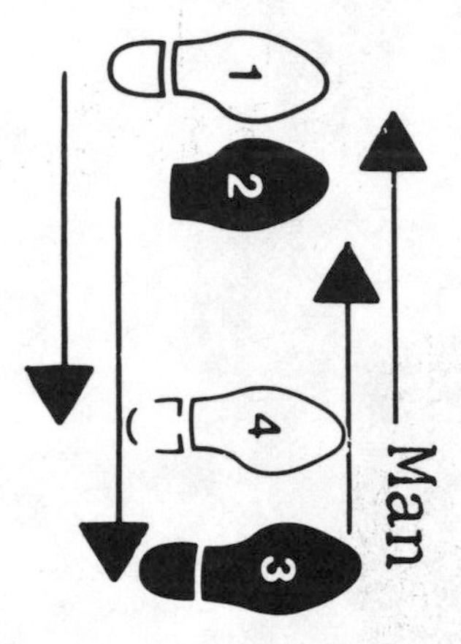

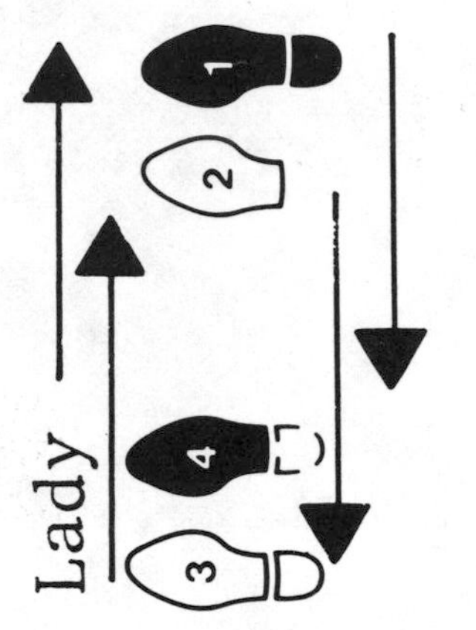

To do the first unit of the sideward hesitation, the man leans to the left and gives a palm lead, then steps to the side of his left. To do the second unit, he counterbalances right and gives a palm lead, then steps to the side with his right foot and touches his left foot to the side of his right.

Step	Position	Directions	Hand Lead
Forward Hesitation	Closed	F (tc) F (tc)	Elbow
Backward Hesitation	Closed	B (tc) B (tc)	Palm
Sideward Hesitation	Conversation	Sd (tc)	Palm
		Sd (tc)	Palm
Front Cross	Conversation	Bk (fr)	Heel
		Fr (bk)	
Back Cross	Conversation	Fr (bk)	Fingers
		Bk (fr)	
Front Hesitation	Conversation	Bk (fr)	Heel,
		Bk (fr)	Fingers
Back Hesitation	Conversation	Fr (bk)	Fingers
		Fr (bk)	Heel

In the front cross the man leans to the left and gives a heel lead, then steps back as he moves to the side and touches his right foot in front of his left. Maintaining his leftward leverage, he then crosses with his right foot and touches his left foot behind his right. In the back cross the man leans to the left and gives a finger lead, then steps in front as he moves sideward and touches his right foot behind his left. He then crosses with his right foot and touches his left foot in front of his right.

Front Cross

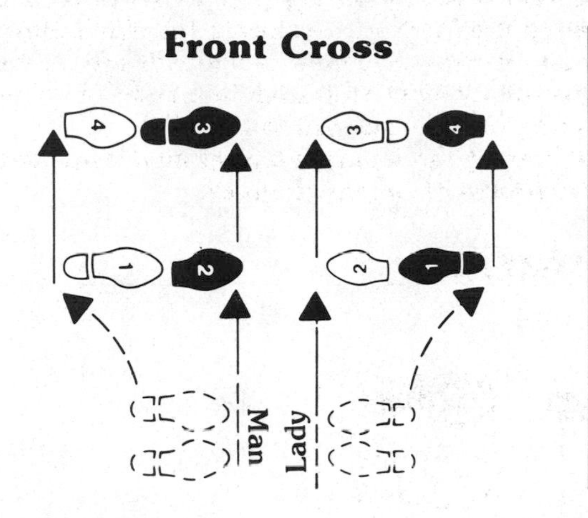

Back Cross

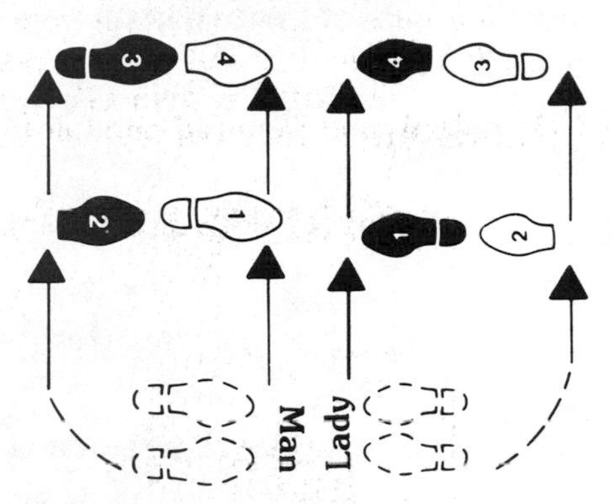

The first unit of the front hesitation is identical to the first unit of the front cross. However, instead of continuing to the left, the man counterbalances to the right and gives a heel lead, then steps in front with his right foot and touches his left foot in back of his right.

Just as in the sideward steps of the walk rhythm and the chasse' rhythm, the lady usually does the same footwork, but the man can have her do opposite footwork by giving her the opposite hand leads.

Front Hesitation

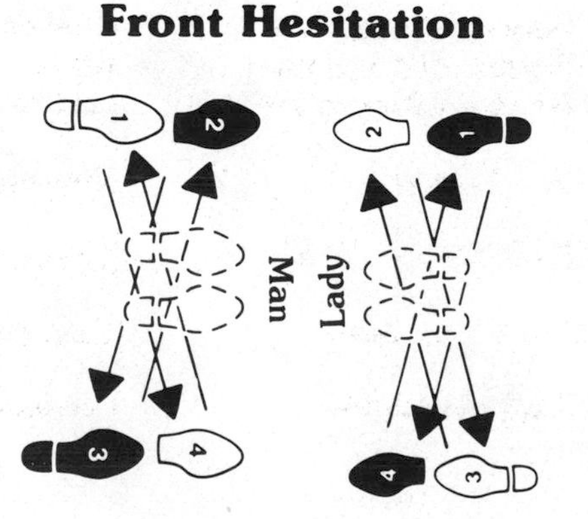

Back Hesitation

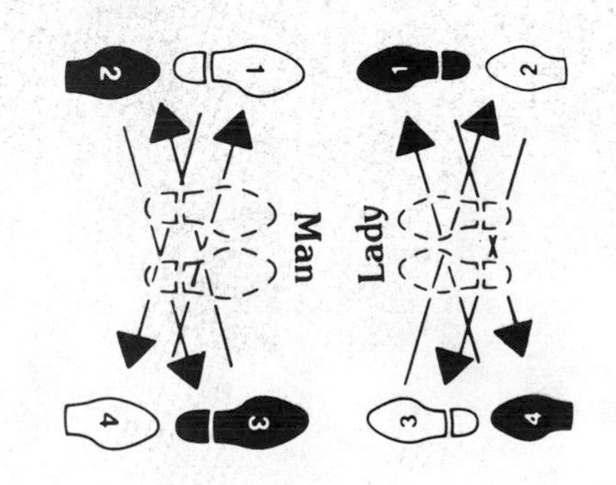

FOXTROT MAGIC

Combining two slow steps with two quick steps.

Magic rhythm is Slow, Slow, quick, quick, taking a measure and a half to complete one step. Capital letters in the Step Pattern Column get a slow count, small letters get a quick count.

Name of Step	Position	Directional Call And Step Description	Man's Hands Leads
Basic Preparation Steps			
Magic Forward	Closed	F F sd tg	Elbow, Palm
Backward Rock	Closed	B F sd tg	Palm, Elbow
Forward Rock	Closed	F B sd tg	Elbow, Palm
Magic Backward	Closed	B B sd tg	Palm

Forward Walk

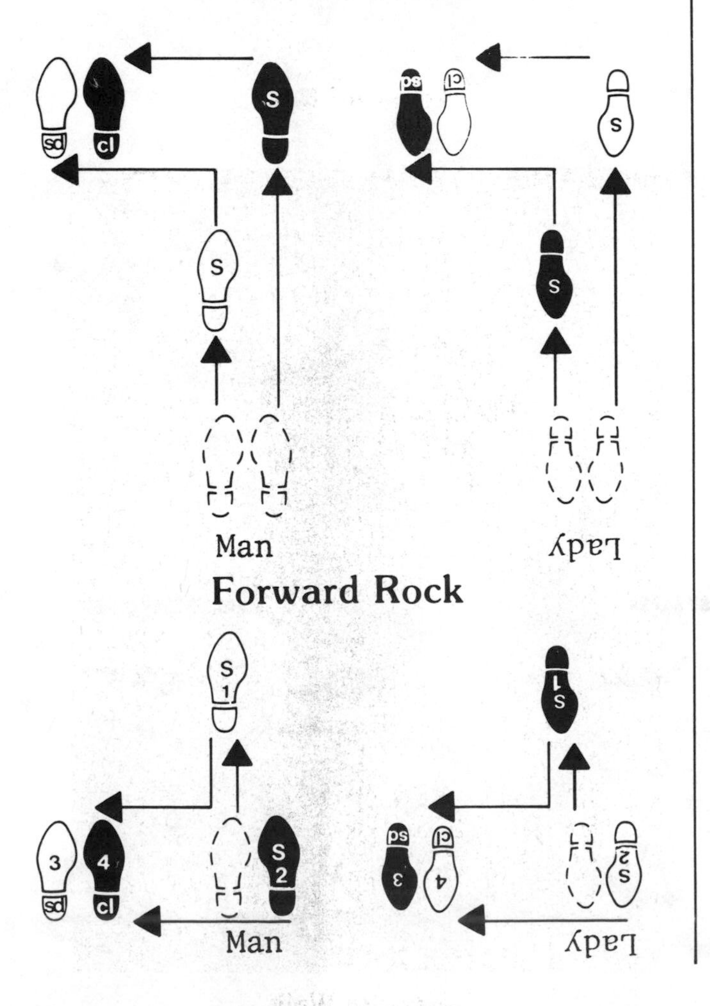

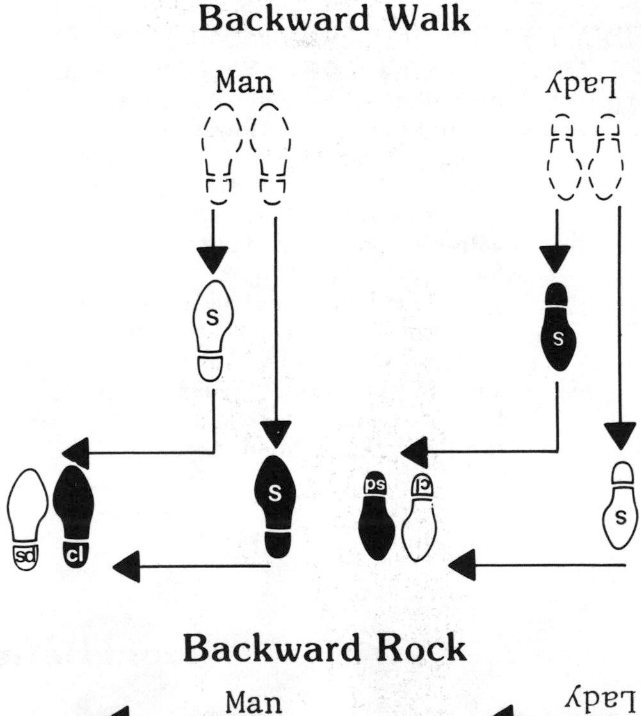

Backward Rock

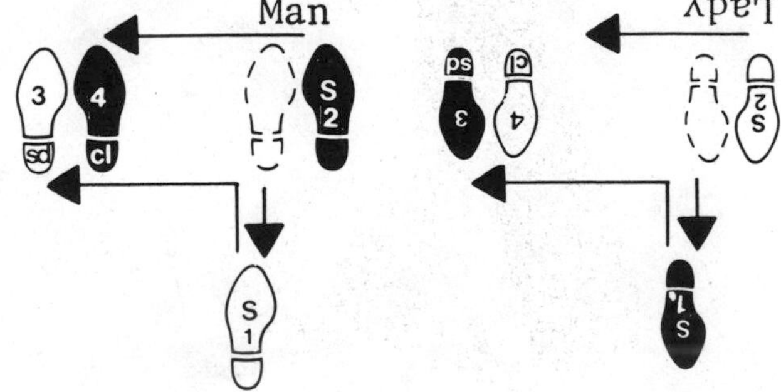

Forward Rock

Backward Rock

Forward Walk

Backward Walk

Step	Position	Directions	Body Lead	Hand Lead
Right Rock Turn	Closed	B F {tr 1/4} sd cl Rpt 3 times	Sh Back, Fwd Left	Heel, Elbow Palm
Left Rock Turn	Closed	F B {tl 1/2} sd cl Rpt 3 times	Sh Fwd, Bwd Left	Fingers, Palm Palm

Right Rock Turn

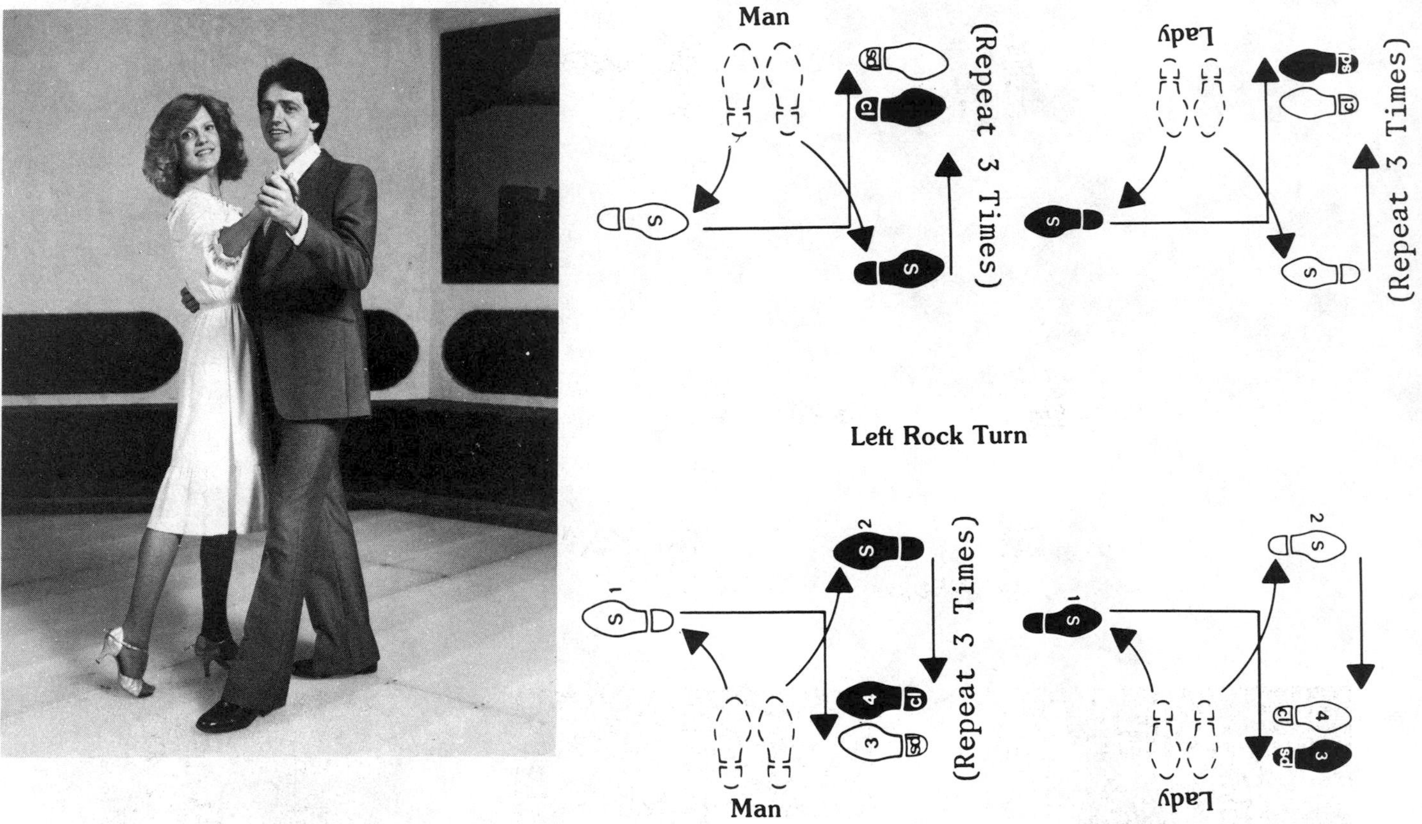

Name of Step	Position	Directional Call And Step Description	Man's Hand Leads
Magic Forward	Closed	F F sd tg	Elbow, Palm
Magic Forward	Right Side to Conversation	F F sd tg (TR ¼)	Elbow, Heel
Magic Back	Left Side to Conversation	B B sd tg (TL ¼)	Palm Fingers
Magic Forward	Semi-open to Conversation	F F sd tg (TR ¼) G Same (TL ¼)	Palm, Fingers
Magic Sideward	Conversation	SdX(F) sd tg G Same	Heel, Palm
Magic Sideward	Reverse to Conversation	B B sd tg (TL ¼) G Same (TR ¼)	Fingers
Magic Forward	Open	F F sd tg (TR ¼) G Same (TL ¼)	Palm, Fingers

Changing Positions with the magic step

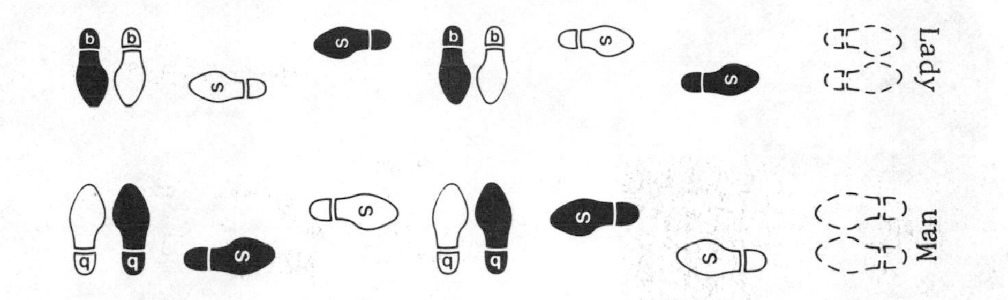

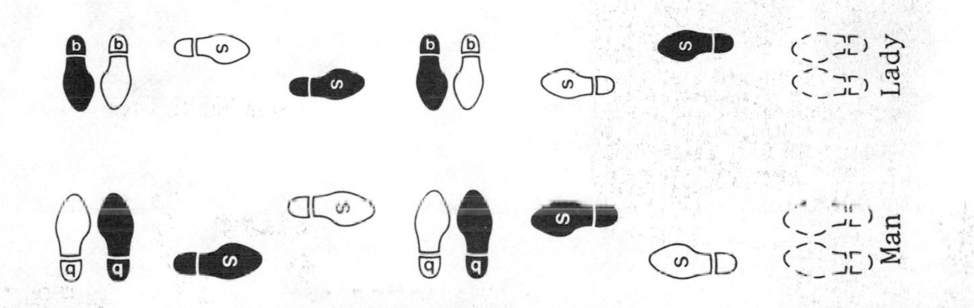

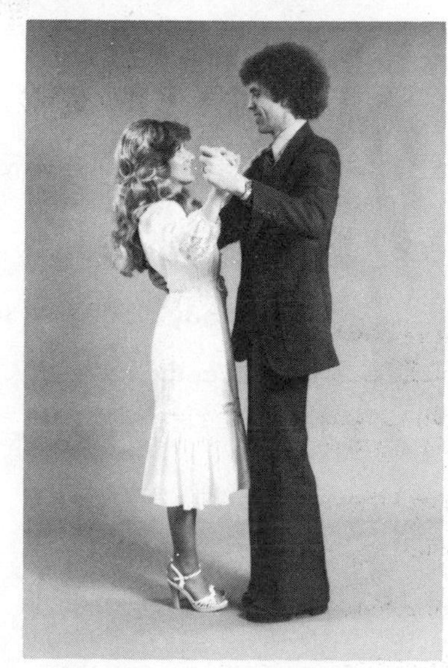

SWING STEP

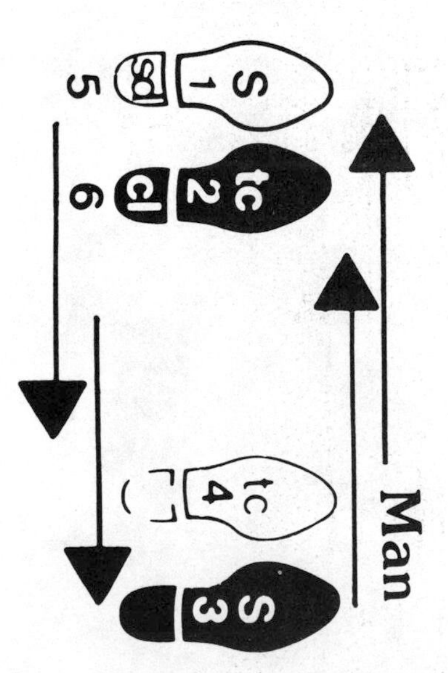

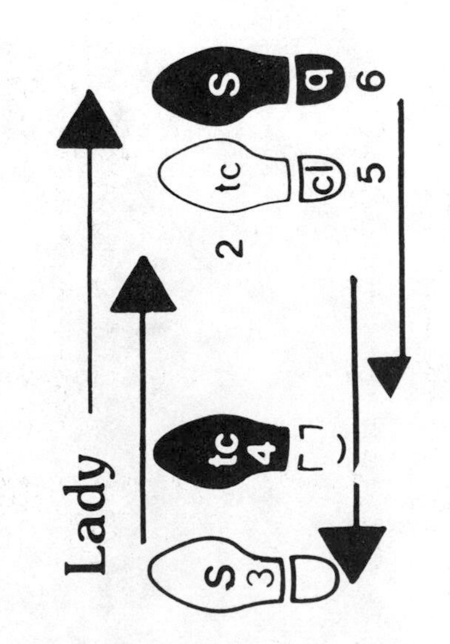

Name of Step: Swing Step

Position: Conversation

Description: Sd(tc)Sd(tc)sd tg

Men's Hand Lead: Palm

Swing Cross	Conversation	Sd(tc)Sd(tc)sd x(F) G Same	Palm, Heel
Swing Cross	Conversation Right Side	Sd(tc)Sd(tc)sd x(F)	Palm, Fingers
Swing Cross	Conversation Left Side	Sd(tc)Sd(tc)sd x(B)	Palm, Heel
Swing Cross	Conversation Reverse	Sd(tc)Sd(tc)sd x(B) G Same	Palm, Fingers
Swing Cross	Conversation Semi-open	Sd(tc)Sc(tc)sd x(F) G Same	Palm, Heel

Conversation position to semi open

Conversation to reverse

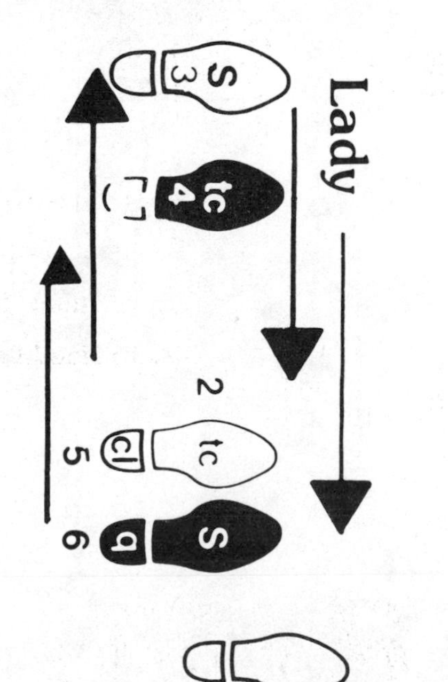

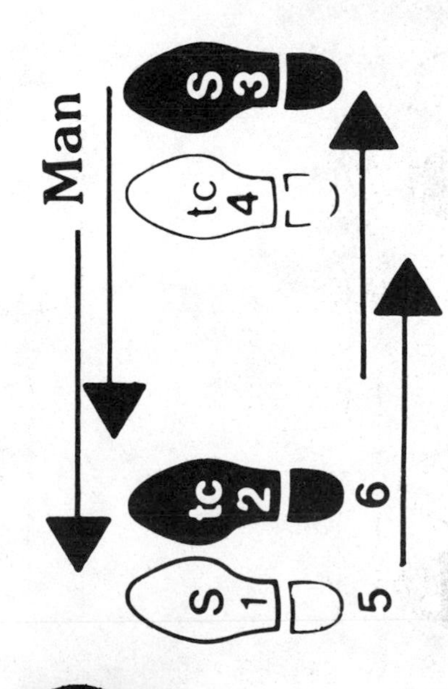

Step	Position	Directions	Hand Lead
Forward Arch	Semi-open L R Cnt	F F @ F B {tr 1} f f @ f b {*tr 1*}	L H High L H High
Backward Arch	Semi-open L R Cnt	B B @ B F {tl 1} b b @ b f {tl 1}	L H X High L H X High

Forward

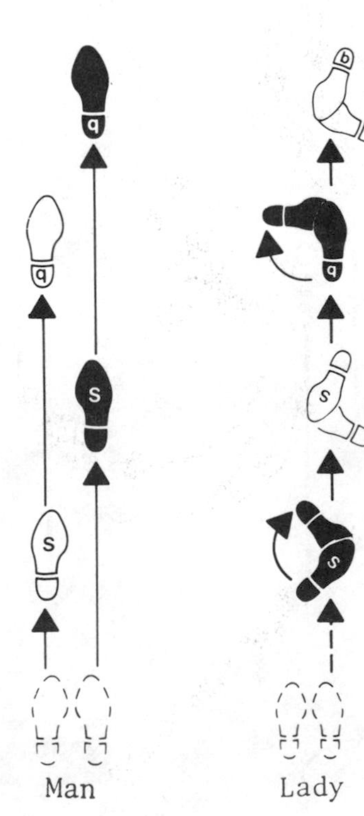

Backward

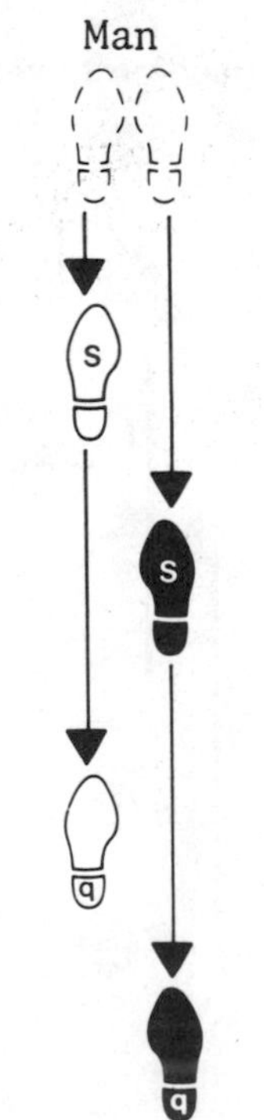

Lady

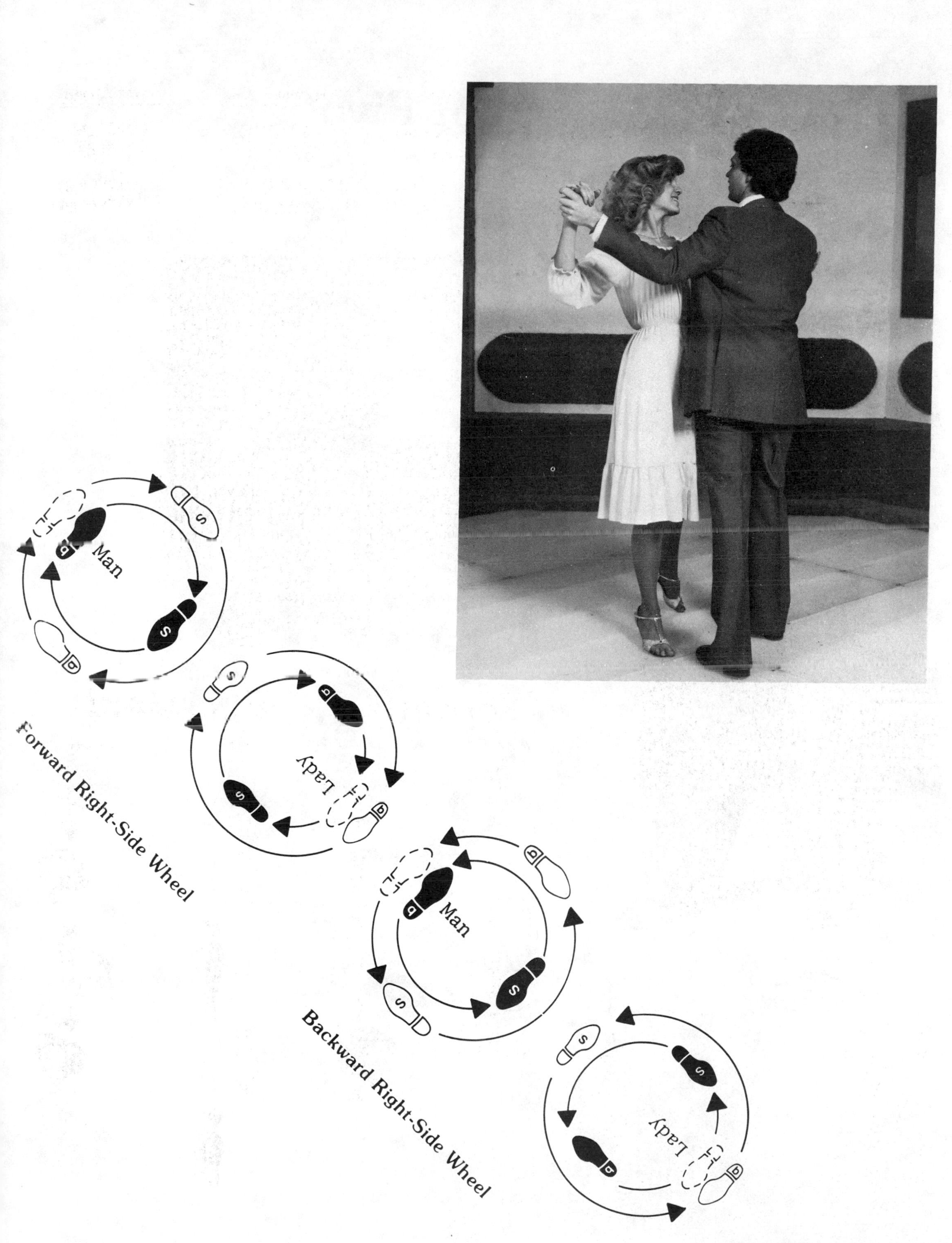
Man
Lady
Man
Lady
Forward Right-Side Wheel
Backward Right-Side Wheel

Right Spot Pivot

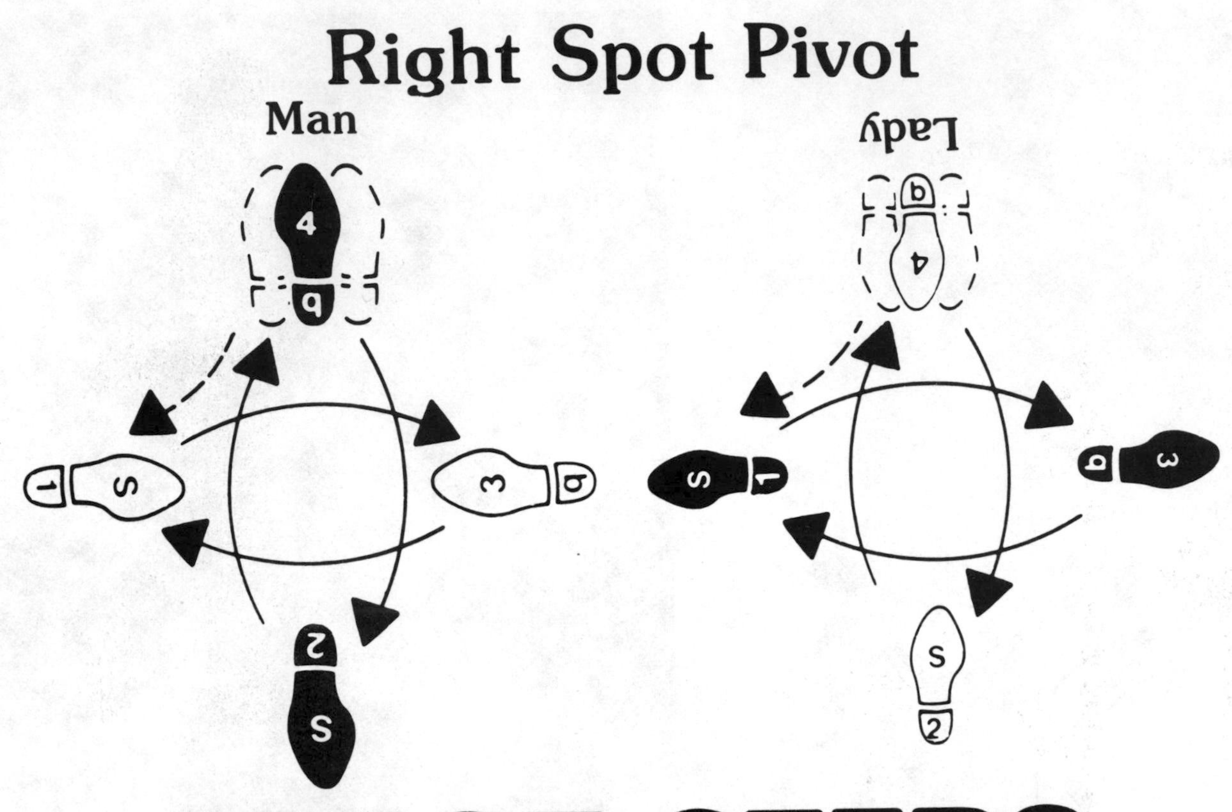

PIVOT STEPS

Left Spot Pivot

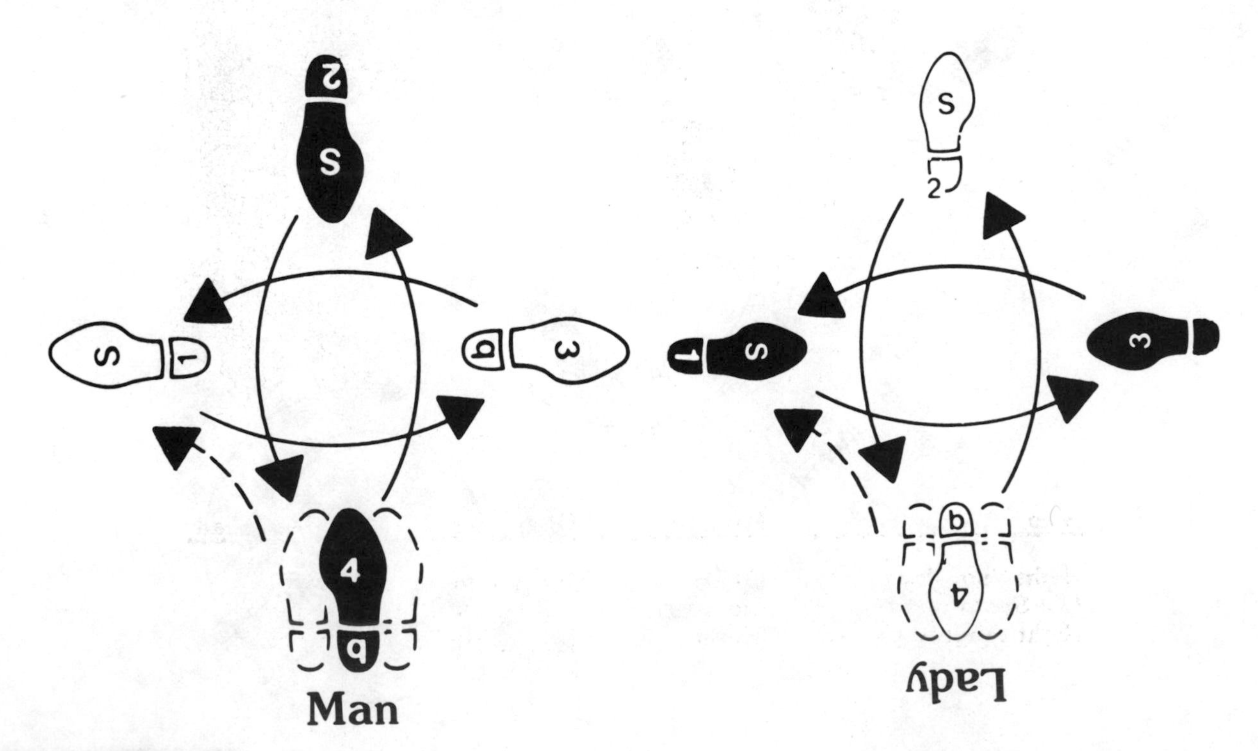

Right Progressive Pivot

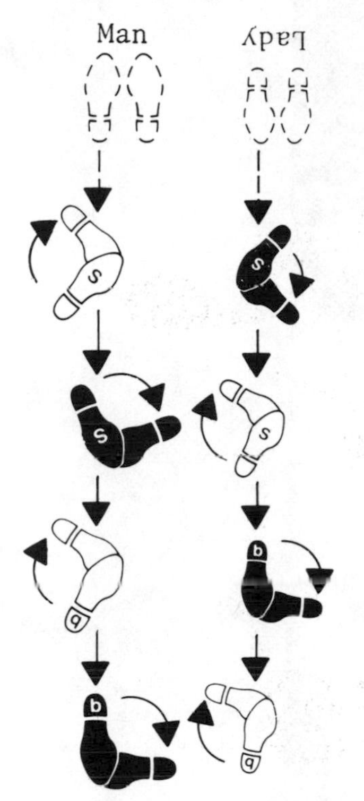

Left Progressive Pivot

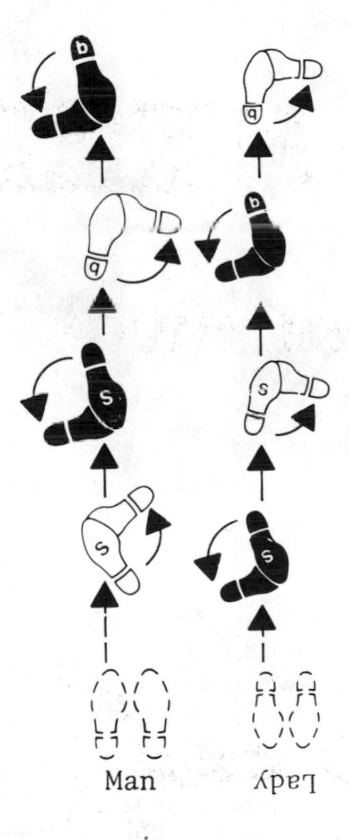

Step	Position	Directions	Hand Lead
Right Spot Pivot	Closed	B F b f {tr 1}	Heel
Left Spot Pivot	Closed	F B f b {tl 1}	Fingers
Right Progressive	Closed	B F b f {tr 2}	Heel

LINDY

The most memorable event in 1927 was the airplane flight of Charles A. Lindbergh from New York to Paris. This unprecedented feat captured the imagination of all the world, and young Lindbergh became the great American hero of his time. It was not at all surprising, then, that a new dance fad should be called the Lindbergh Hop. This was later shortened to the Lindy Hop and finally to Lindy. This is the Lindy that is still danced today.

The origin of this foxtrot novelty is obscure. Some say it was first danced by some sailor boys and their girl friends; others claim an African origin, while still others suggest this or that professional teacher as originator. Whatever its beginnings might have been, it spread like wild-fire when it was named the Lindbergh Hop. It became so popular that contests were held and groups traveled from state to state to compete in them.

Before long a related but extremely acrobatic form of the hop came on the scene. This new fad combined the Lindy, the Charleston, the Black Bottom, the Big Apple and a tumbling act all into one. The wilder the antics of the dancers, the more proficient it was necessary to be. This new craze soon became tagged with the name "Jitterbug." Jitterbug has now become disco.

BASIC SEMI-OPEN STEPS

When in semi-open position, both the man and the lady first step straight forward and back and the lead is palm. When dancers dance the sideward basic, position. On the second slow movement, the couple step sideward then return to semi-open position on the quick movements. The finger lead is used to get into conversation position; the heel of the right hand is used to get back into semi-open position.

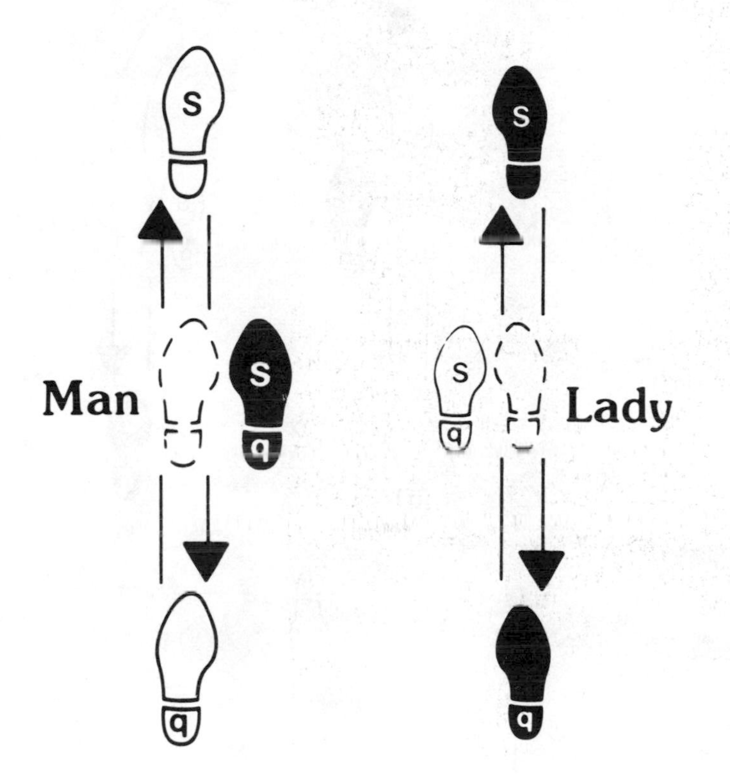

Step	Position	Directions	Hand Lead
Semi-open Basic	Semi-open	F B @ F B b f @ b f	Palm

Style

Elbows should never by fully extended but should always retain a slight bend to give an elastic action. Avoid excessive arm movements. Body and arms should move as one. Resistance is important for good leads and quick responses. Ladies should keep fingers "cupped" so that their hands don't easily slip away from man's grasp. Keep your body and knees relaxed. This will aid in developing the "loose," relaxed Lindy style.

Semi Open Sideward

Semi-open	Semi-open	FR {tr 1/4} @	Fingers
Sideward		FR {tl 1/4} B {tl 1/4} @ B {tr 1/4} b f @ b f	Heel Palm
Walk In	Full-open SO L R Contact	F B b f G FB b f(TR 1/2)	Drop R Hand
Walk Out	Semi-open F L R Contact	F B b f G FB b f(TL 1/2)	Drop R Hand

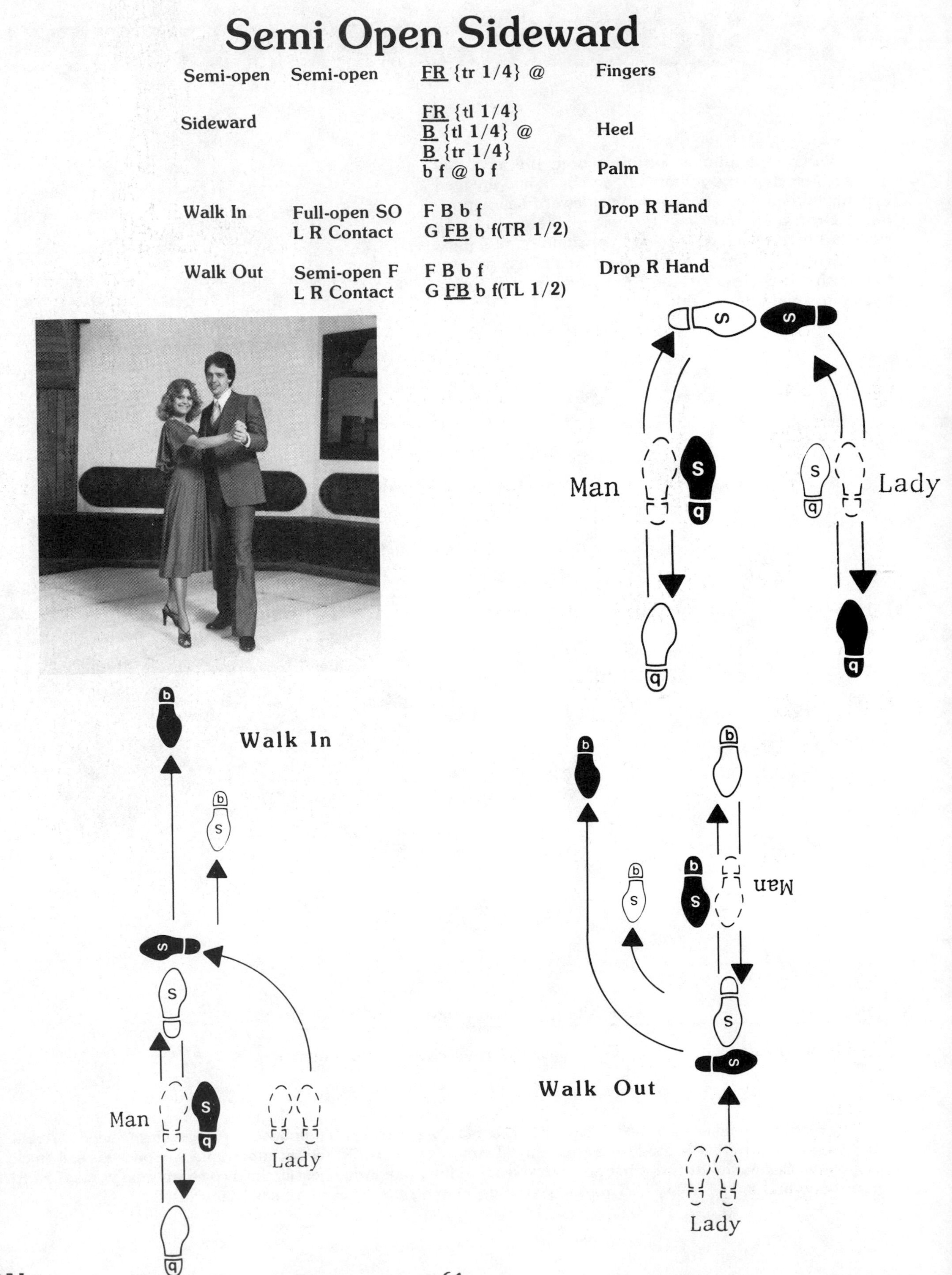

When learning the basic lindy step in two-hand position, dancers step forward toward each other on the first movement (slow). The man starts on his left foot; the lady, on her right foot. The man pulls his partner directly forward with both hands. The second slow movement is in place as the weight is shifted to the right foot. The left foot for the man is then placed behind the right foot, and the weight is momentarily changed from the right to the left foot, then back to the right.

Two Hand Basic	2 H Fc to Fc	F B b f G Same	Both H Low

TWO-HAND BASICS

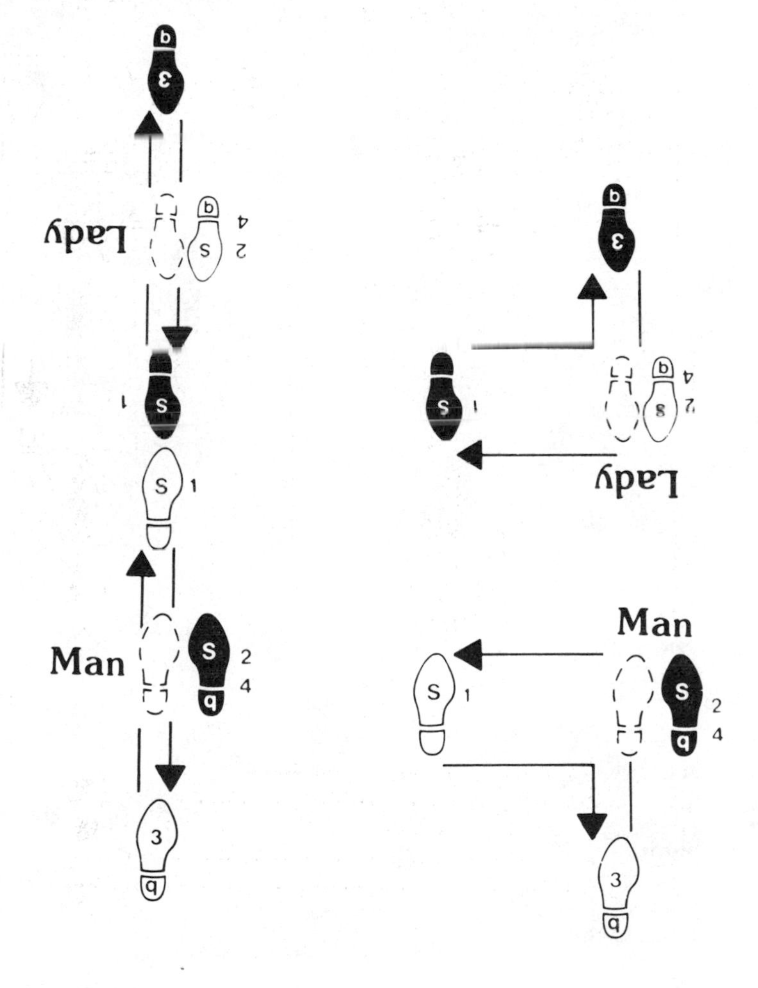

In dancing the sideward basic the first movement is directly sideward, with the left foot for the man and right foot for the lady. The third movement is straight back, left foot for man, right foot for lady; and the fourth movement is in place, right foot for man and left foot for lady.

COMBINATION STEPS

Arch In

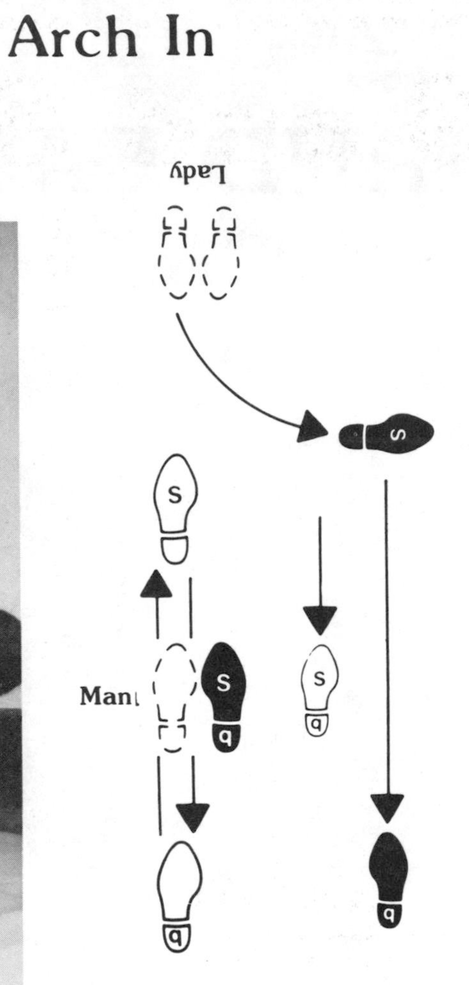

Arch Out

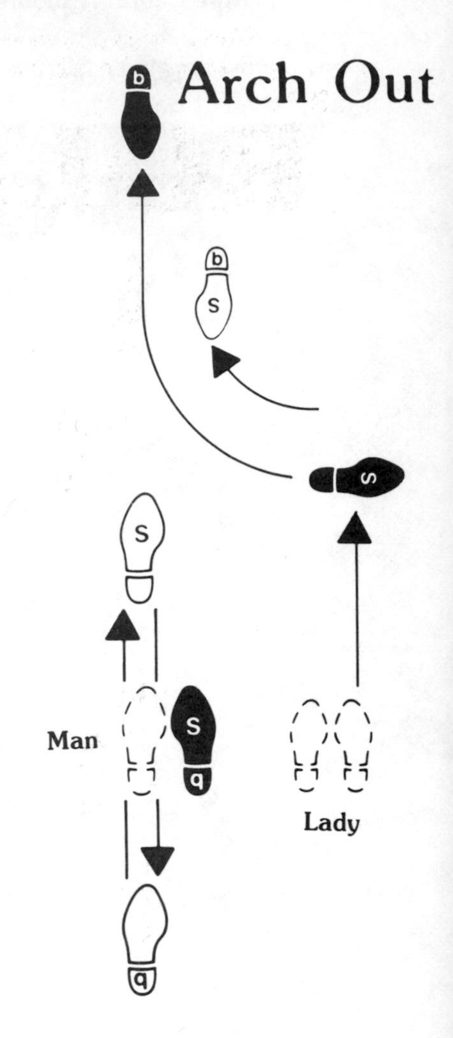

Step	Position	Directions	Hand Lead
Arch In	Two Hand, LR Cnt Semi-open	F B @ FB {tl 1/2} b f @ b f	LH High
Arch Out	Two Hand, RR Cnt	F B @ FB {tr 1/2} b f @ b f	LH High
Roll In	Two Hand, RR Cnt Skaters	F B @ FB {tl 1/2} b f @ b f	Take RH
Roll Out	Skaters, RR Cnt Two Hand	F B @ FB {tr 1/2} b f @ b f	Drop LH
Spin In	LR Cnt, Shine Semi-open	F B @ FB {tl1/2} b f @ b f	Cross LH Low Throw
Spin Out	Semi-open, Shine Two Hand	F B @ FB {tr 1/2} b f @ b f	Tuck, LH Fist

The difference between rolls and spins is indicated by the man's lead. If the man holds a lady's hand low during the step it is a roll or walk. If he holds his hand high it is an arch. If the man throws and releases the lady's hand, it is called a spin. A spin is preceded with a tuck, which means the lady is tucked in close to the leader before spinning.

The man pulls the lady gently into a tuck on the first slow movement, then pushes her into a spin on the second slow movement. The lady places her weight on the right foot in the tuck and keeps the weight on the right foot in the spin.

ROLLS and SPINS

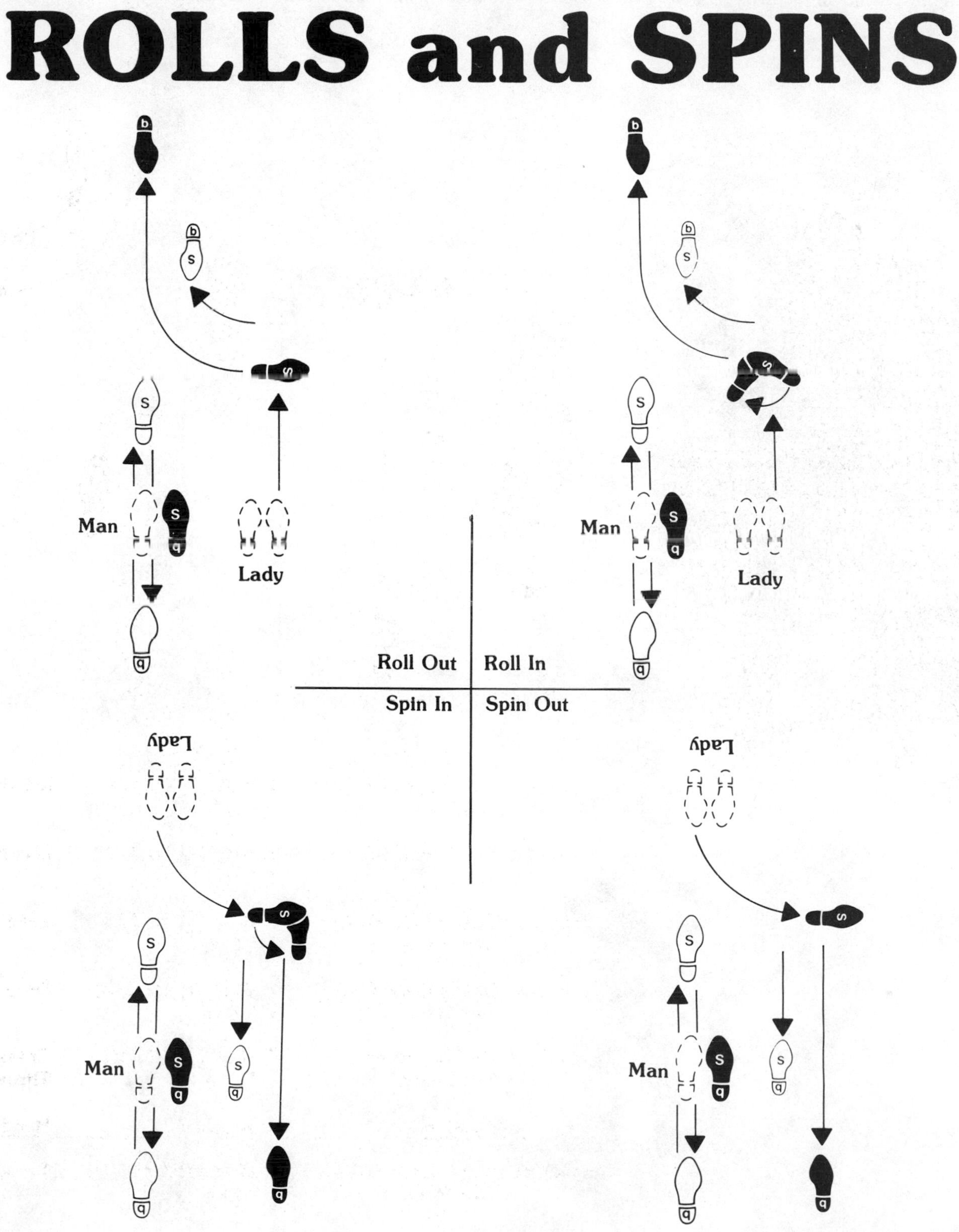

Double Spin

Double Spin. Partners stand face to face, L R contact.

Man and lady step forward toward each other on the first slow and both push against their partner, turning one complete turn. Man turns left; lady turns right. The step is finished in shine position.

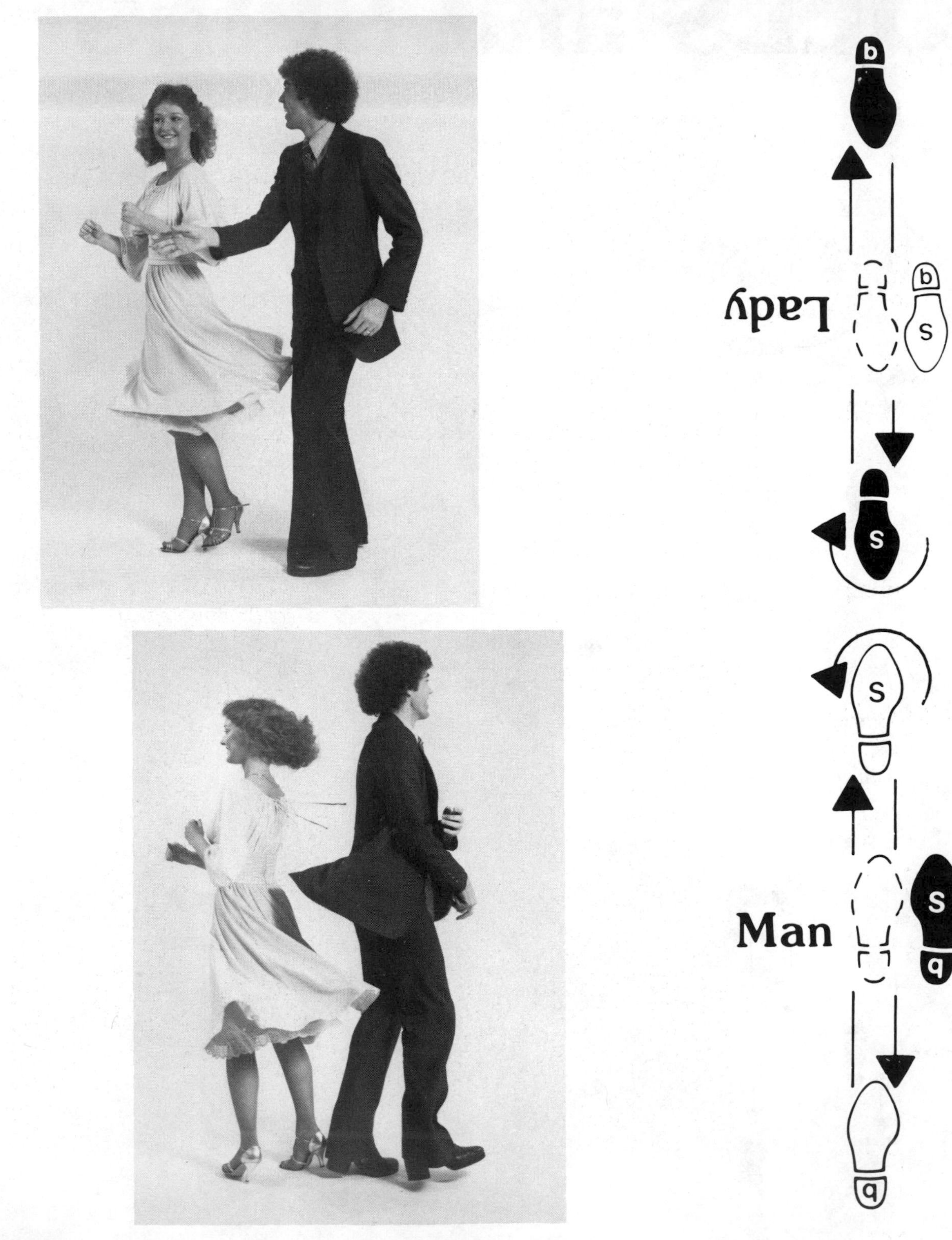

Right Semi-open Turn	Semi-open	F B @ F B {tr 1/2} b f @ b f Rpt	Sh Back, Bwd Bwd, Fwd	Heel Palm Fingers
Left Semi-open Turn	Semi-open	F B @ F B {tl 1/2} b f @ b f Rpt	Fwd, sh Fwd Bwd, Fwd	Fingers, Palm Heel

Right Semi-Open Turn

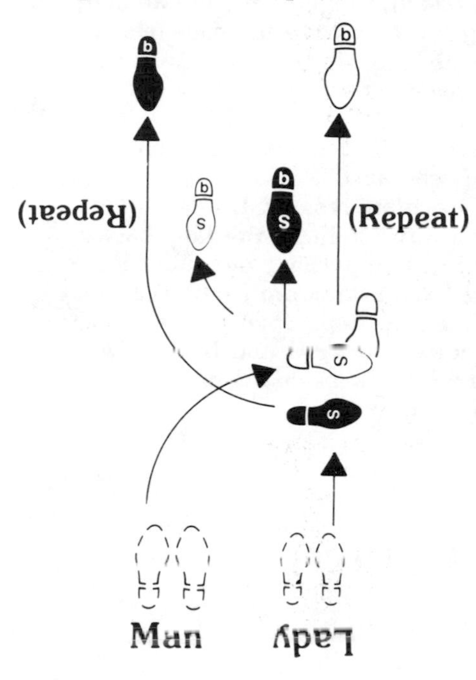

Left Semi-Open Turn

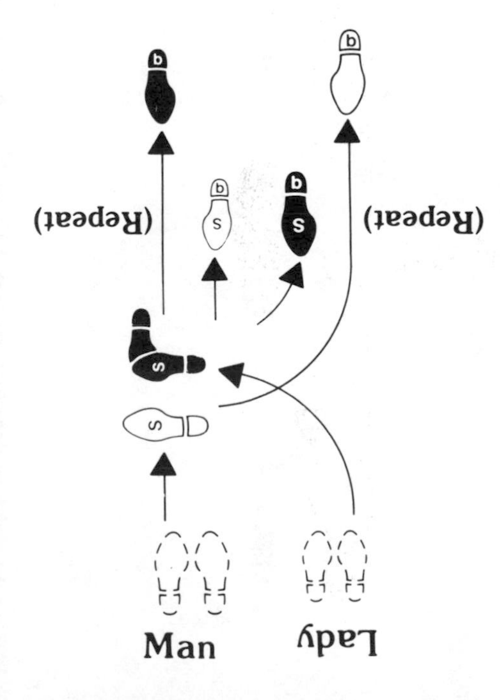

FORWARD & BACKWARD ARCH

Forward Arch. Partners stand face to face, L R contact.

The man raises his left hand, and the lady moves forward under the arch and turns right one-half, changing places with her partner.

The man steps forward with his left foot (slow), turning left one-half and stepping back on his right foot (slow), and rocking back and forward on the quick movements.

Backward Arch. Partners stand face to face, L R contact.

The man crosses his left hand high and turns right as the lady backs under the arch, turning one-half left. Partners back away from each other on the second slow step. Then rock in place (quick quick), forward and back. The lady's hand turns inside the man's hand as they arch.

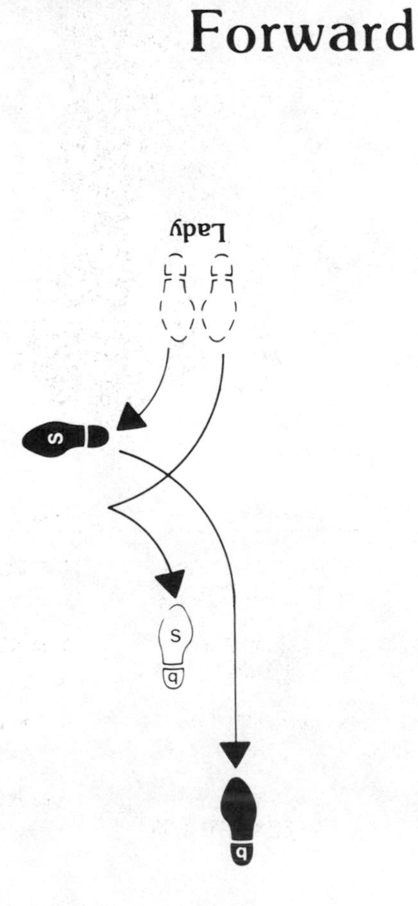

Backward

b
b
S
S
Lady
S
S
b
b
Man

Left-Hand Walk Around. Partners stand face to face, L R contact.

The man turns left one-half, turning his back on his partner and releasing hands as he passes his partner, then joining hands on the quick movements. The lady turns right one-half as she changes places with her partner.

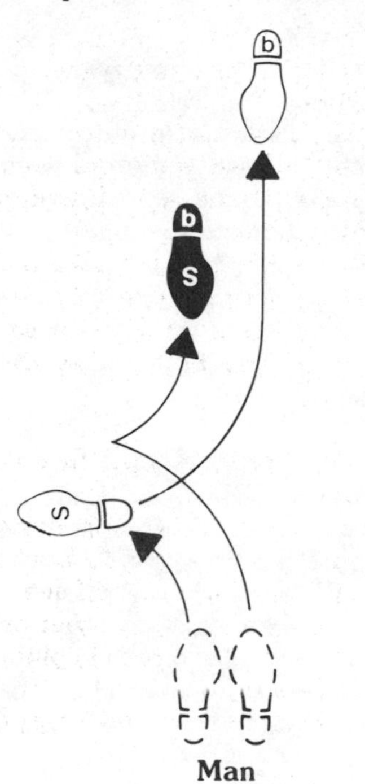

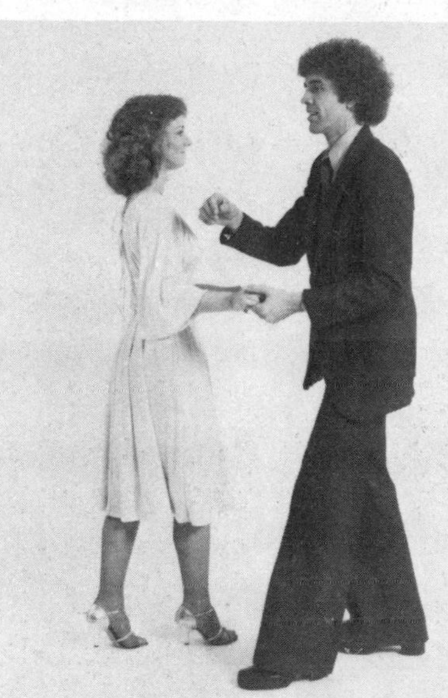

Lady

Right-Hand Walk Around. Partners stand face to face, R R contact.

The man places his right hand on the back of the lady's right hand and turns left one-half back to back with partner. As the man turns, he places the lady's right hand in his left hand. The lady turns left one-half and does the same footwork as she did on the left-hand walk around.

Steps	Position	Direction	Hand Lead
Forward Arch	Full-open L R Contact	FB b f(TL 1/2) G FB b f(TR 1/2)	L H High
Backward Arch	Full-open L R Contact	BB b f(TR 1/2) G BB b f(TL 1/2)	L H X High
L H Walk Around	Full-open Shine L R Contact	FB b f(TL 1/2) G FB bf(TR 1/2)	L H Low
R H Walk Around	Full-open R R Contact	FB b f(TL 1/2) G FB b f(TR 1/2)	Join R Hands

Changing Positions

Left-Hand Roll to Cuddle

The man holds his left arm out, then joins his free hand after the lady rolls into roll position. The man drops his right hand to indicate to the lady that she should roll out to two-hand position.

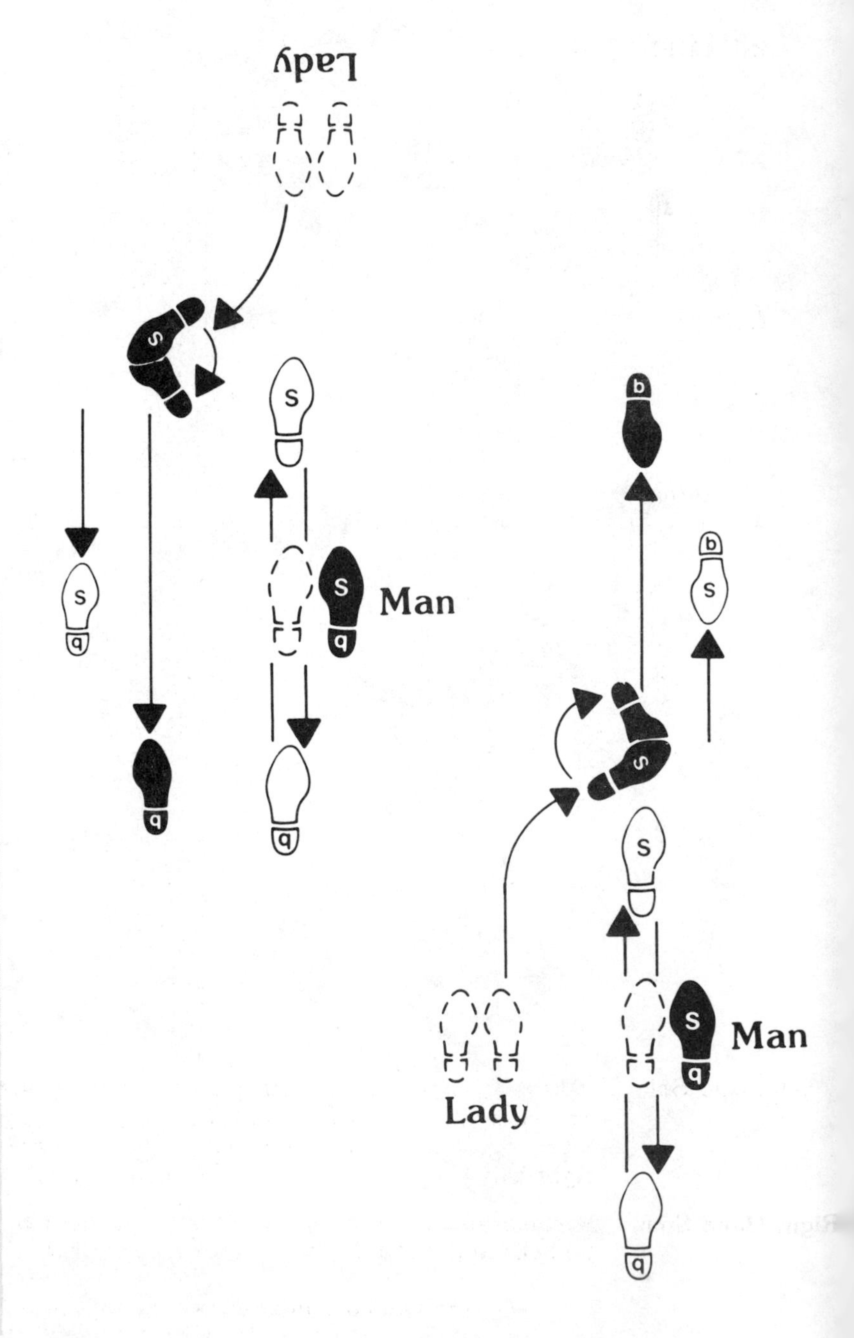

Step	Position	Direction	Hand Lead
LH Roll to Cuddle	Two Hand, LR Cnt	F B @ FB {tr ½}	LH Out
	Left Cuddle	b f @ b f	
LH Roll Out	Left Cuddle, LR Cnt	F B @ FB {tl ½}	Drop RH
	Two Hand	b f @ b f	
LH Spin	LR Cnt, Shine	F B @ FB {tr 1}	LH Fist
	Two Hand	b f @ b f	
RH Spin	RR CNt, Shine	F B @ F B {tr 1}	RH Fist
	Two Hand	*b f* @ b f	

Left-Hand Spin

Right-Hand Spin

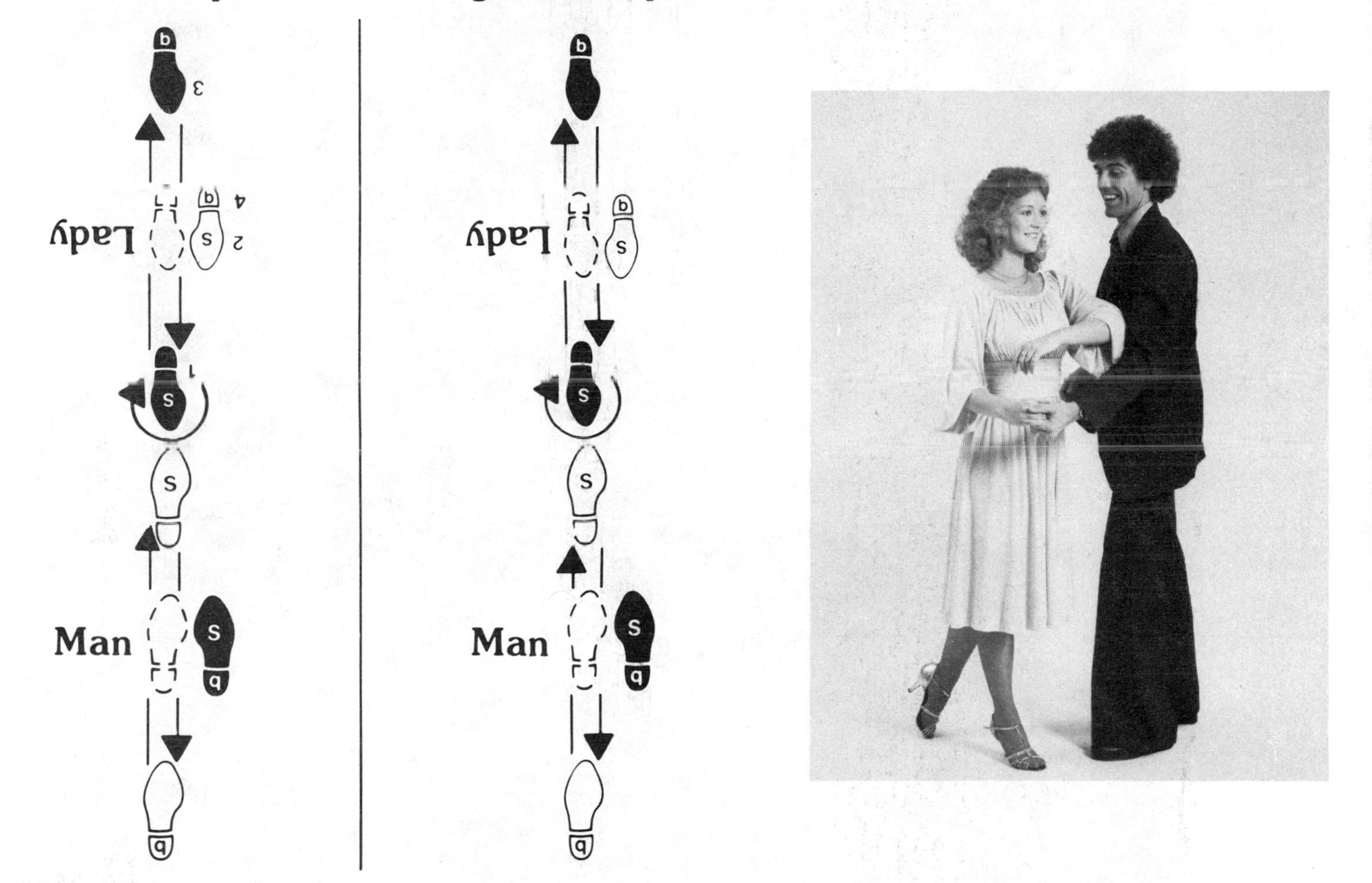

Left-Hand Spin — Man faces lady, L R contact. The man makes a fist with his left hand and pulls the lady forward on the first slow step. On the second slow step, the man pushes with his left hand and the lady spins one complete turn to the right on her right foot. Partners join hands, L R contact, and rock back (quick) on the right foot.

Right-Hand Spin — Partners stand face to face, R R contact. The man makes a fist with his right hand. On the first slow step he pulls and tucks the lady onto her right foot.

On the second slow step, the lady spins on her right foot one complete right turn. Partners again join hands R R contact and rock back (quick), then forward (quick).

The waltz has been called the "queen of dances." It is the oldest of our ballroom dances and has had a strong influence upon the aesthetics of other types of dances. In colloquial German, walzen means "gliding" or "sliding."

The waltz originated in Austria or Switzerland during the middle of the eighteenth century. At first it was considered a daring dance because of the close contact between partners. But as the years passed, it became not only acceptable, but fashionable. The music of Johann Strauss gave the waltz tremendous popularity.

Forward Basic Box

The step patterns of the box rhythm in the waltz are identical to the step patterns of the box-step rhythms in the foxtrot and the rumba. The major difference is the music count. Whereas a unit of box-step rhythm consists of a slow step and two quick steps in 2/4 time, a unit of box rhythm in the waltz consists of three slow steps in 3/4 time. Just as in the box-step rhythms of the foxtrot and the rumba, each unit of the box rhythm is composed of an optional forward, backward, or sideward step followed by a mandatory sideward chasse'. To do the first unit, the man takes a step with his left foot, then does a right chasse'; to do the second unit, he takes a step with his right foot, then does a left chasse'. The lady's footwork is counterpart to the man's.

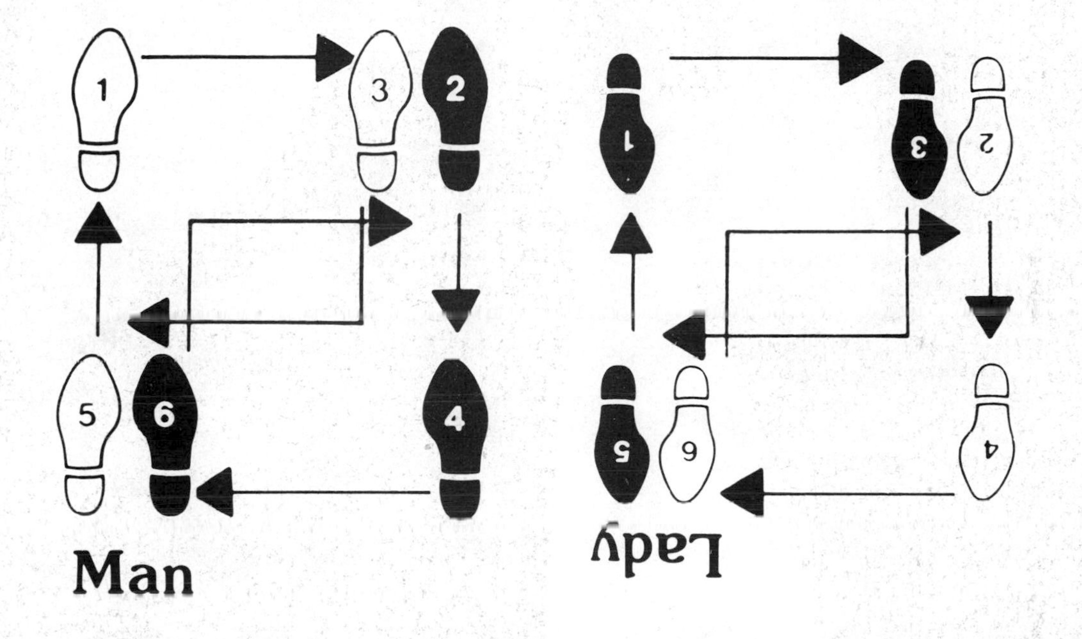

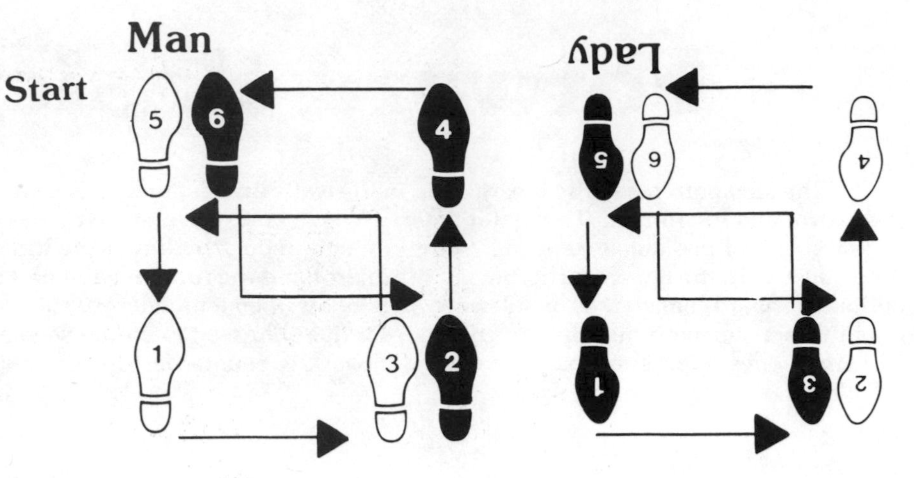

Style

- The posture is erect.
- The movement is smooth and continuous.
- Use "rise and fall" to give expression to the 3/4 timing. (This is the down, up, up" motion which accents the 1 count on the "down," then continues to rise on counts 2 and 3.) The motion is carried out by the whole body. The body exhibits rising action by stretching through the torso. Use the legs by bending the knees slightly on the first count, commencing to straighten at the end of count 1, rising on the secong and third counts until the whole body is up. Lower at the end of count 3, as the backward step is taken.

Forward Box	Closed	F Sd Tg-B Sd Tg	Elbow, Palm
Progressive Forward Waltz	Closed	F Sd Tg-F Sd Tg	Elbow
Left Box Turn	Closed	F Sd Tg-B Sd Tg (TL 1/2) Repeat	Fingers
Progressive Backward Waltz	Closed	B Sd Tg-B Sd Tg	Palm
Backward Box	Closed	B Sd Tg-F Sd Tg	Palm
Right Box Turn	Closed	B Sd Tg-F Sd Tg (TR 1/2) Repeat	Heel

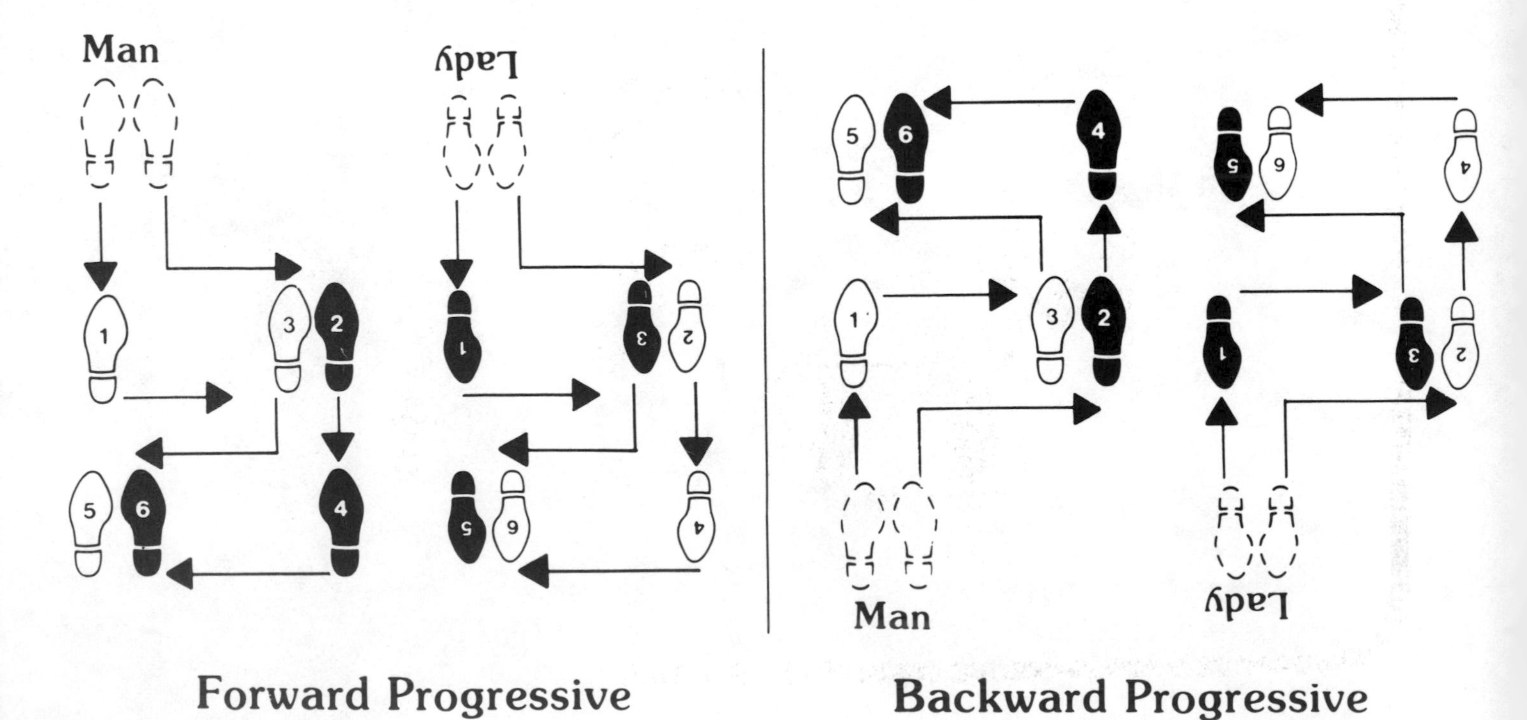

Forward Progressive

Backward Progressive

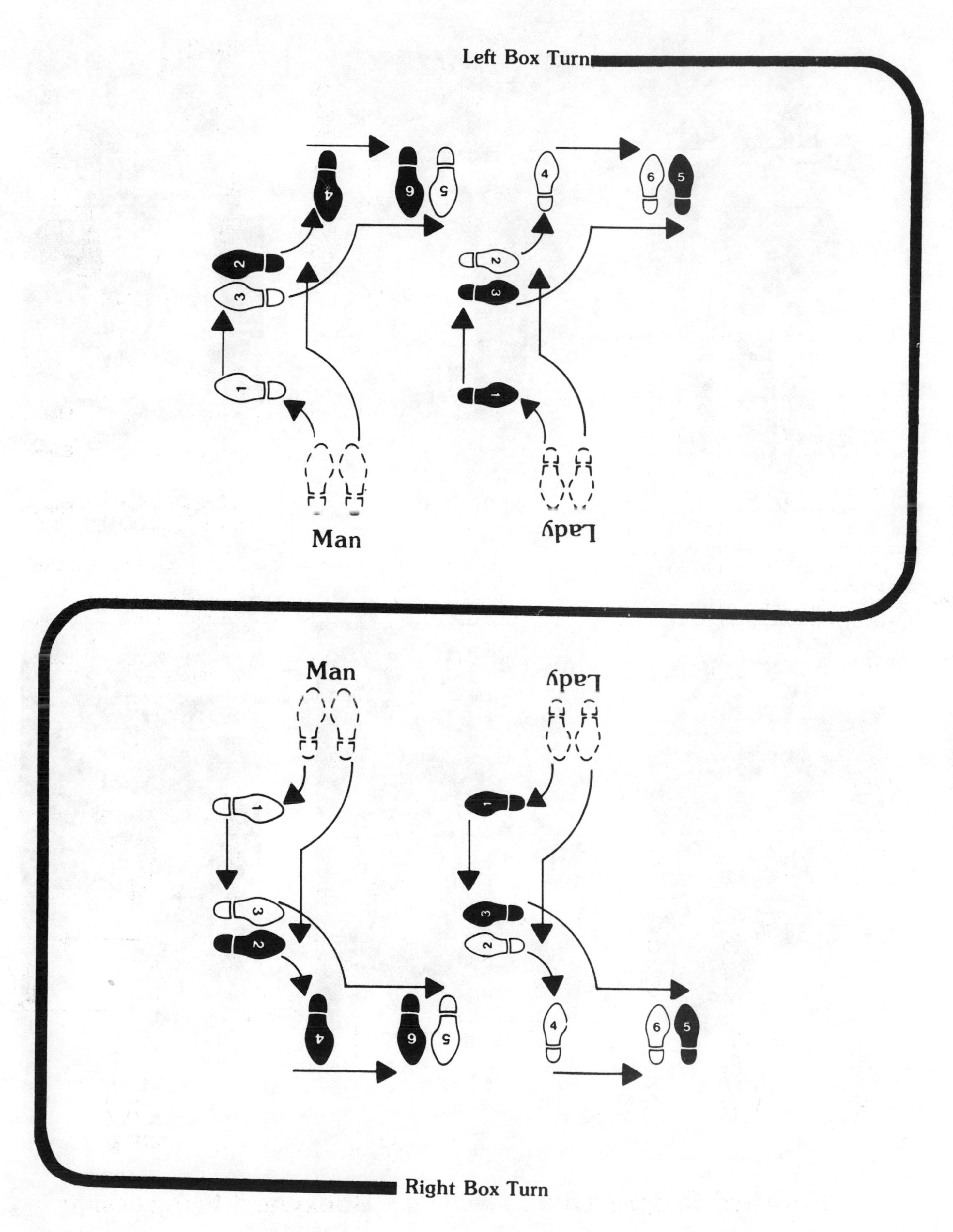
Left Box Turn
Man
Lady
Man
Lady
Right Box Turn

Right Side

Left Side

Semi-Open

Reverse

Open

Closed

Progressive Waltz Steps

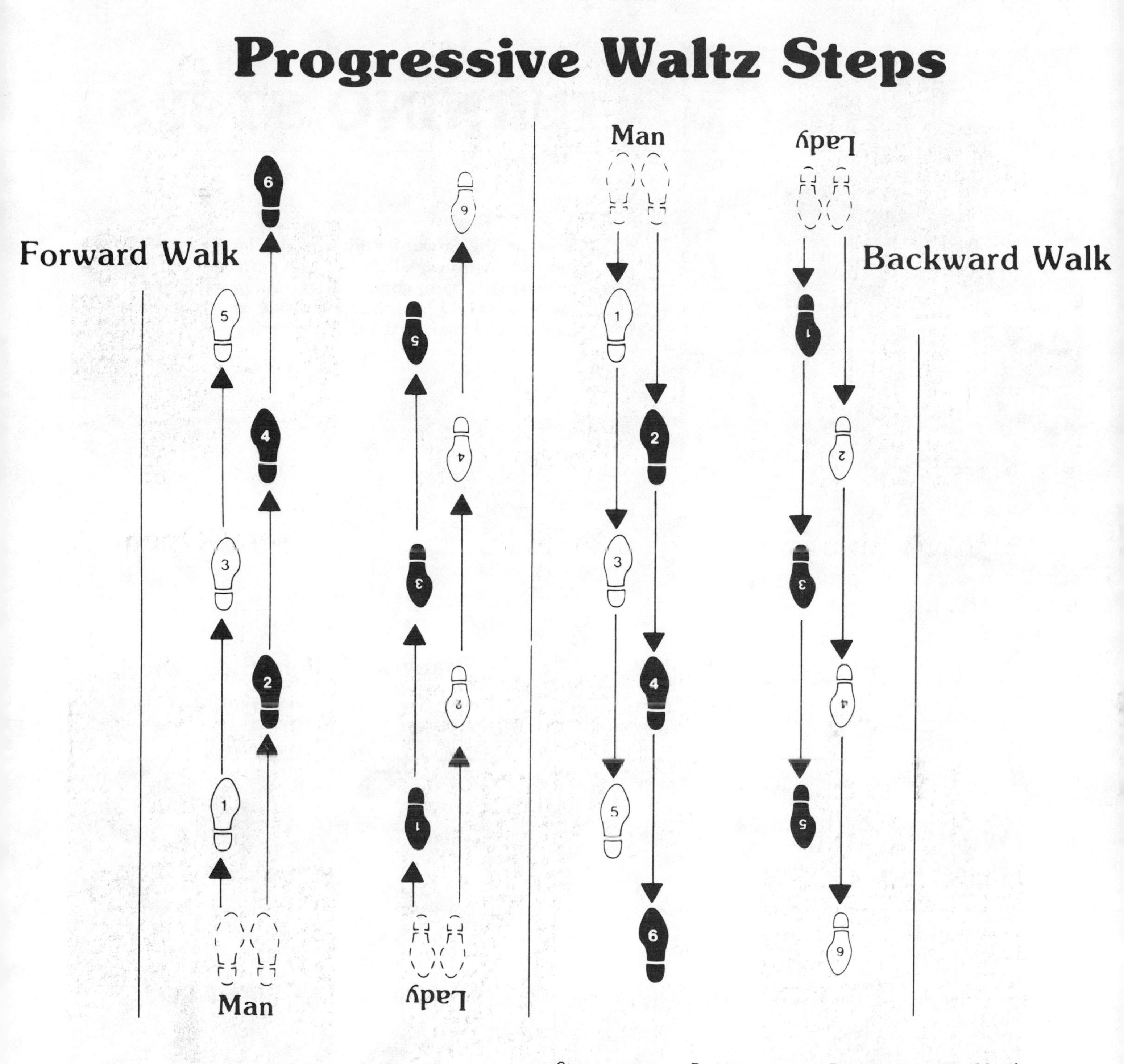

Each measure of the waltz walk rhythm constitutes a separate unit composed of three forward, backward, or sideward steps. As a result, every step pattern takes six beats, or two measures of 3/4 time. The man begins the first unit on his left foot and the second unit on his right. Feet never come together when dancing this step.

Step	Position	Direction	Hand Lead
Progressive Forward Waltz	Right Side	F F F-F F F	Elbow
Progressive Backward Waltz	left Side	B B B-B B B	Palm
Progressive Forward Waltz	Semi-open	F F F-F F F G Same	Palm
Progressive Backward Waltz	Reverse	B B B-B B B G Same	Palm
Progressive Forward Waltz	Open	F F F-F F F G Same	Palm

TURNING STEPS

Because the forward walk and the backward walk have six steps instead of four, both partners must turn one-sixth of a turn, not a quarter turn, on each step of the forward and backward right-side wheels and the forward and backward left-side wheels.

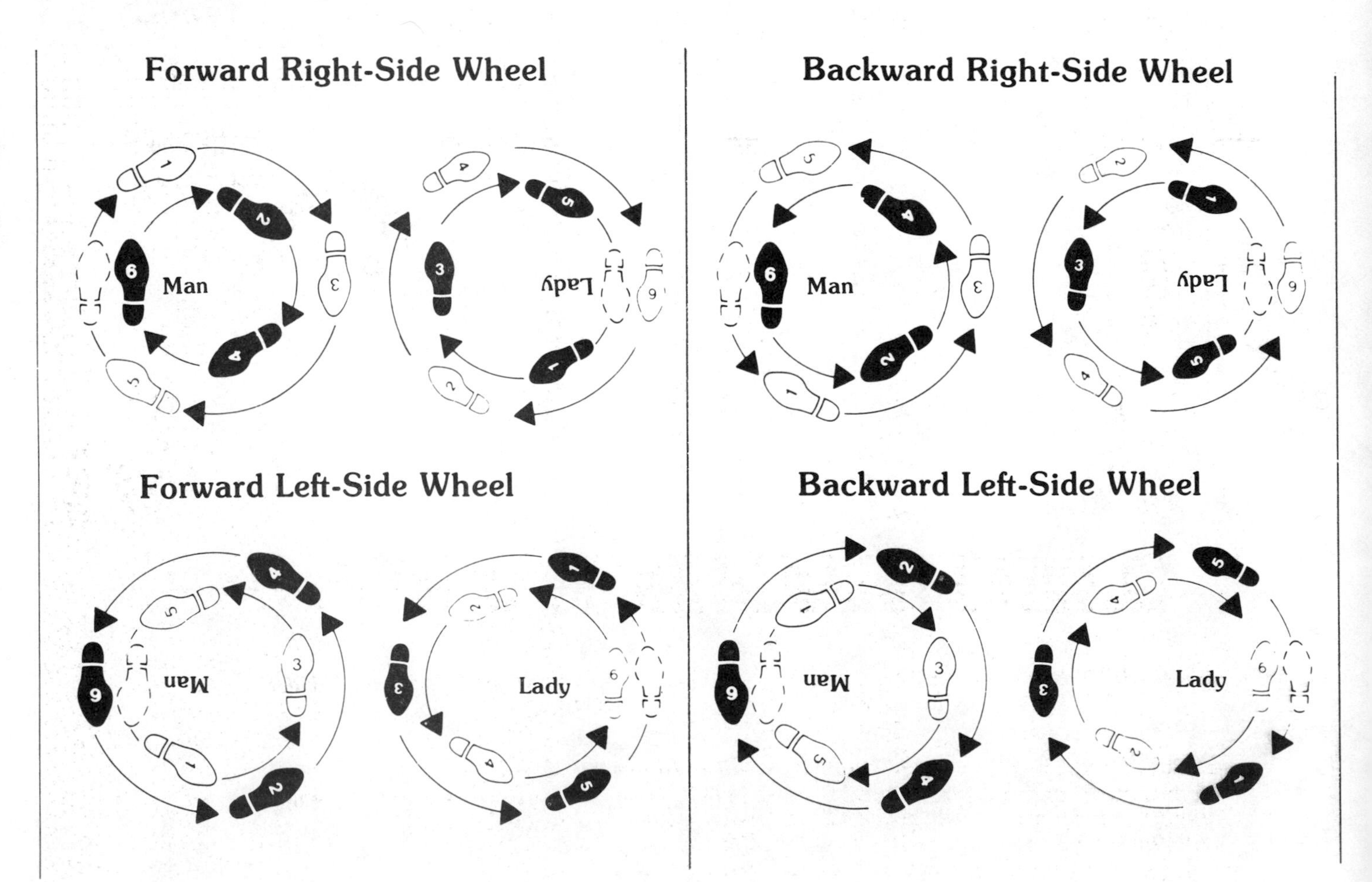

In the first unit of the right spot pivot the man turns right a sixth turn as he steps backward, another sixth turn as he steps forward, and another sixth turn as he steps backward, returning to the starting point facing the opposite direction. In the second unit he takes a forward step, a backward step, and a forward step to return to the starting point. In the first unit of the left spot pivot the man turns left a sixth turn as he steps forward, another sixth turn as he steps backward, and another sixth turn as he steps forward, thus facing opposite the starting point. In the second unit he takes a backward step, a forward step, and a backward step to return to the starting position. Just as in the spot pivots of the collegiate walk.

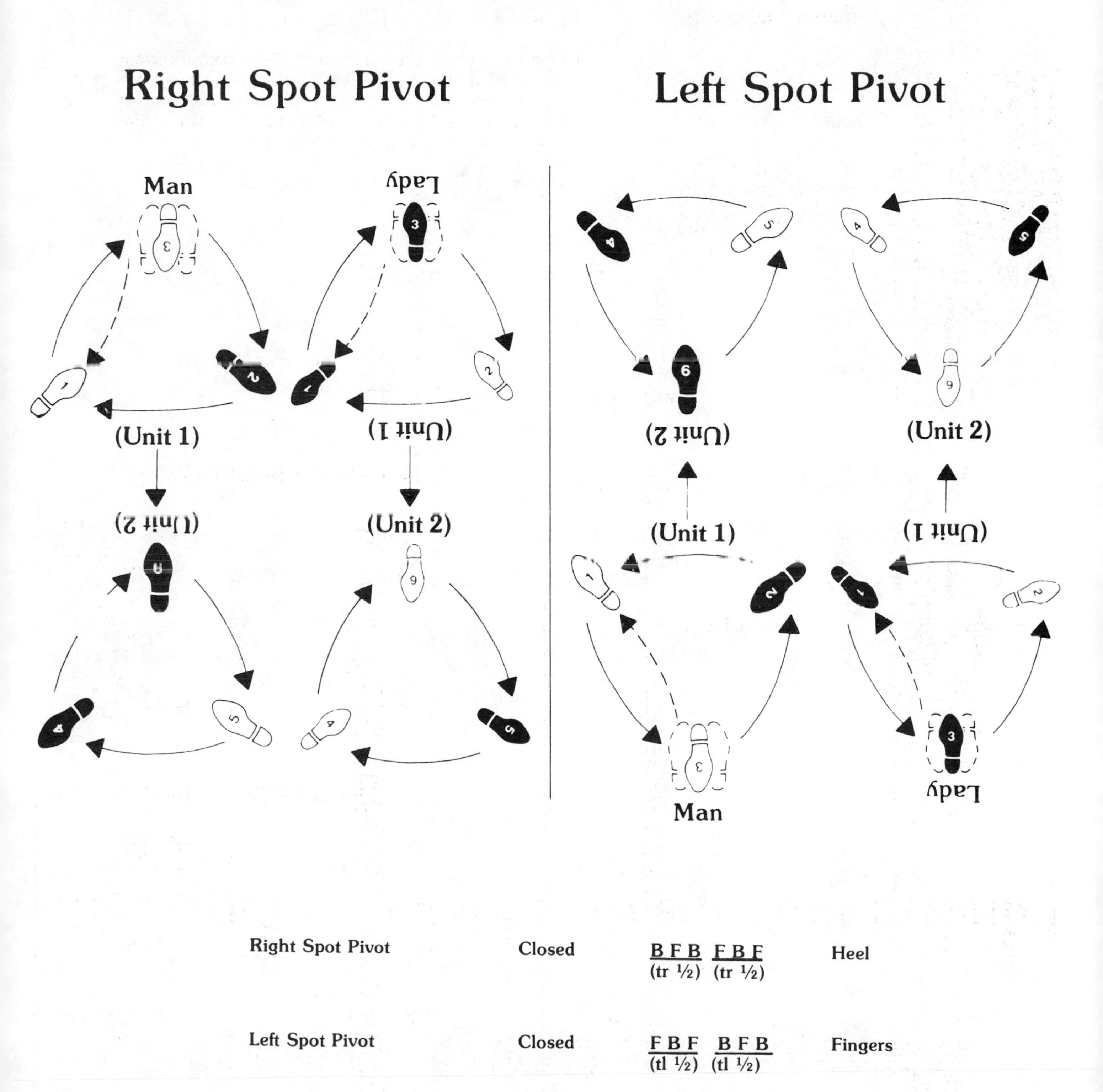

Right Spot Pivot	Closed	BFB FBF (tr ½) (tr ½)	Heel
Left Spot Pivot	Closed	FBF BFB (tl ½) (tl ½)	Fingers

On each step of the right progressive pivot both partners pivot right half a turn. On each step of the left progressive pivot they pivot left half a turn. Just as in the progressive pivots of the collegiate walk, when beginning from the starting position, they must take an eighth-turn lead-off to gain momentum.

Right Progressive Pivot	**Closed**	**B F B** / **(tr 1½)** / **F B F** / **(tr 1½)**	**Heel**
Left Progressive Pivot	**Closed**	**F B F** / **(tl 1½)** / **B F B** / **(tl 1½)**	**Fingers**

PART IV

LATIN RHYTHMS

CHA CHA

Just as the mambo was an outgrowth of the rumba, the cha cha was a provocative variation of the mambo. The cha cha has become one of the most popular Latin American dances ever to invade North America and Europe. The secret of its international appeal is colorful, quick-moving footwork that is fun and easy to perform.

Tempo
Slow cha cha is considered to be from 90 to 110 quarter note counts to the minute; medium cha cha, from 110 to 120; fast cha cha, 120 and up. The slow and medium tempos are more conducive to ballroom dancing

Rhythm and Timing
Just as cha cha is a dance in which many style variations are used to suit individual preferences, the same is true of timing. Cha cha music is written in 4/4 time. Dance rhythm is "SLOW SLOW quick quick SLOW."

Style and Footwork
1. Posture is held upright but has a less formal appearance than in the foxtrot and waltz.
2. Weight should be kept forward over the balls of the feet. Footwork should be sharp and staccato. Pick the feet up by bending the knees slightly, then "spear" the floor with a "ball to heel" action. Footwork is primarily a ballflat action except on backward rock steps. Then the change of direction is made easier, with better balance and control, by reversing the backward momentum with a quick stop. Using a back toe-ball action, shove forward briskly.

3. Dance position is semi-open (approximately 4-8 inches separation) to allow for more freedom of movement. Because of this semi-open position, the right arm and shoulder and left-hand lead will be used.

Forward Basic

Partners stand face to face in two-hand position.

Unit 1. The man moves his left foot forward slow on the first beat, and his right foot backward slow on the second beat, then closes his left foot to his right and marks time on the cha cha count 3 and 4 (quick quick slow).
Unit 2. The man moves his right foot back, places the left foot forward, and then closes the right foot to the left and marks time (quick quick slow). The lady dances opposite footwork, moving back as the man moves forward on the first unit.

Step	Position	Directions	Hand Lead
Forward Basic	Closed	F B tg ba Ch B F tg ba Ch	Elbow Palm

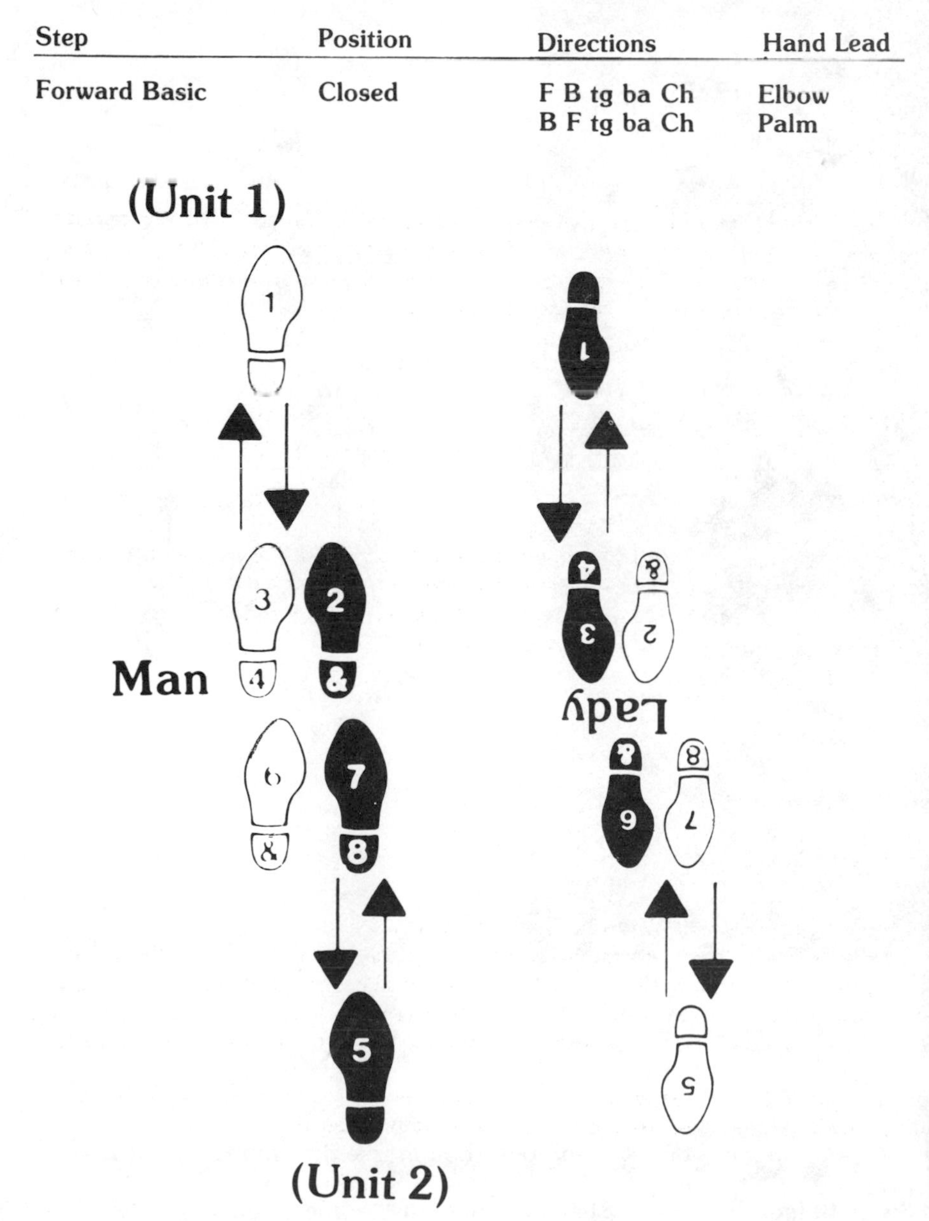

Backward Basic

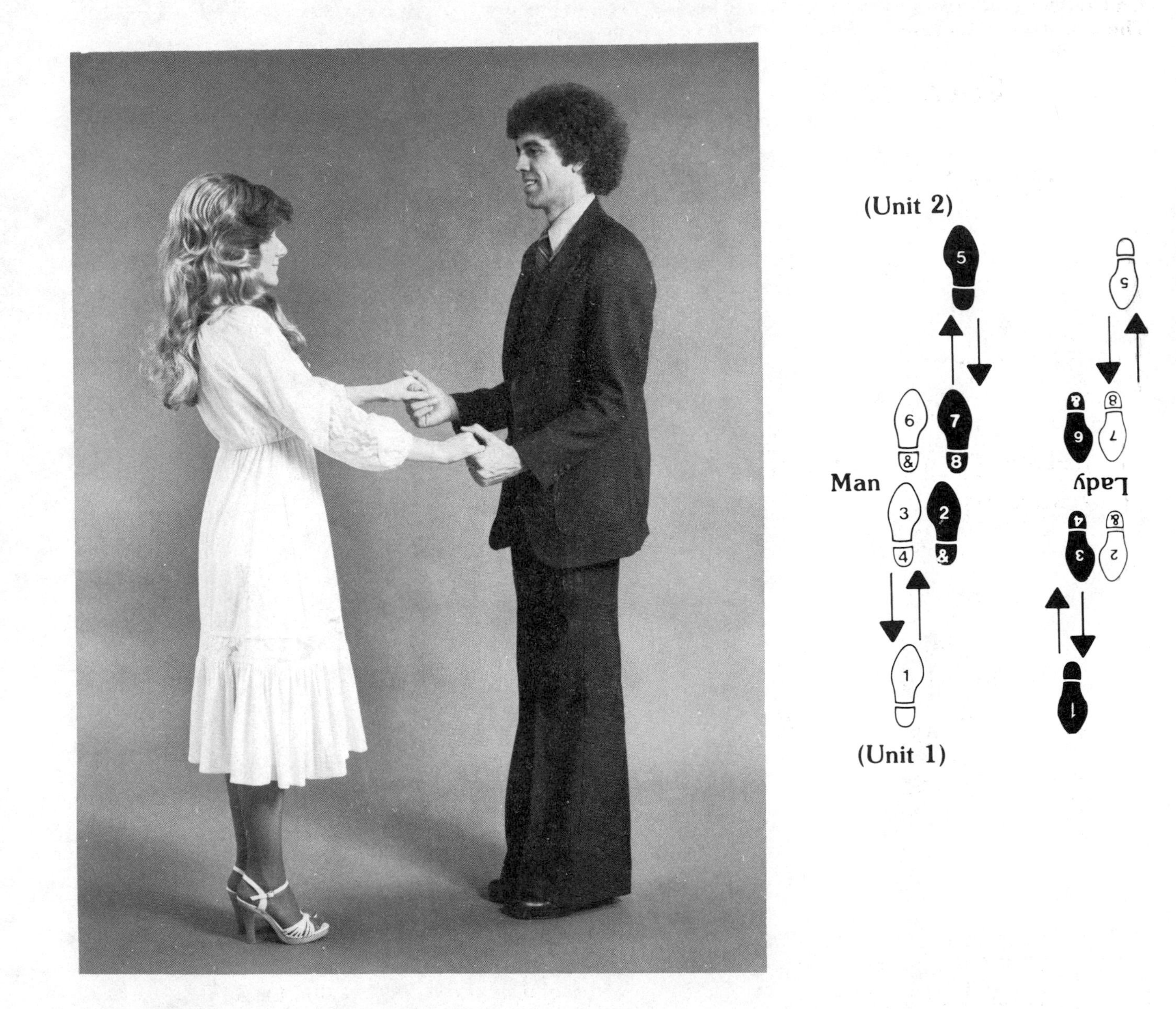

Backward Basic

Partners stand in two-hand position.
Unit 1. The man rocks back on the left foot, forward on the right foot, then marks time in place, L R L (quick quick slow).
Unit 2. The man steps forward on the right foot, back on the left foot, and marks time in place, R L R.
Lady dances opposite footwork.

Forward Break

Unit 1. The man steps forward on the left foot, back on the right foot and steps in place L R L (quick quick slow).
Unit 2. The man steps forward on the right foot, back on the left foot slowly, and marks time in place, R L R. The lady does the same footwork starting on the right foot.

Backward Break

Unit 1. The man steps back on the left foot slowly, forward on the right foot slowly, and marks time on the spot, L R L (quick quick Slow).
Unit 2. The man steps back on the right foot slowly, forward on the left foot slowly and marks time in place R L R. The lady dances the same footwork as the man but on the opposite foot.

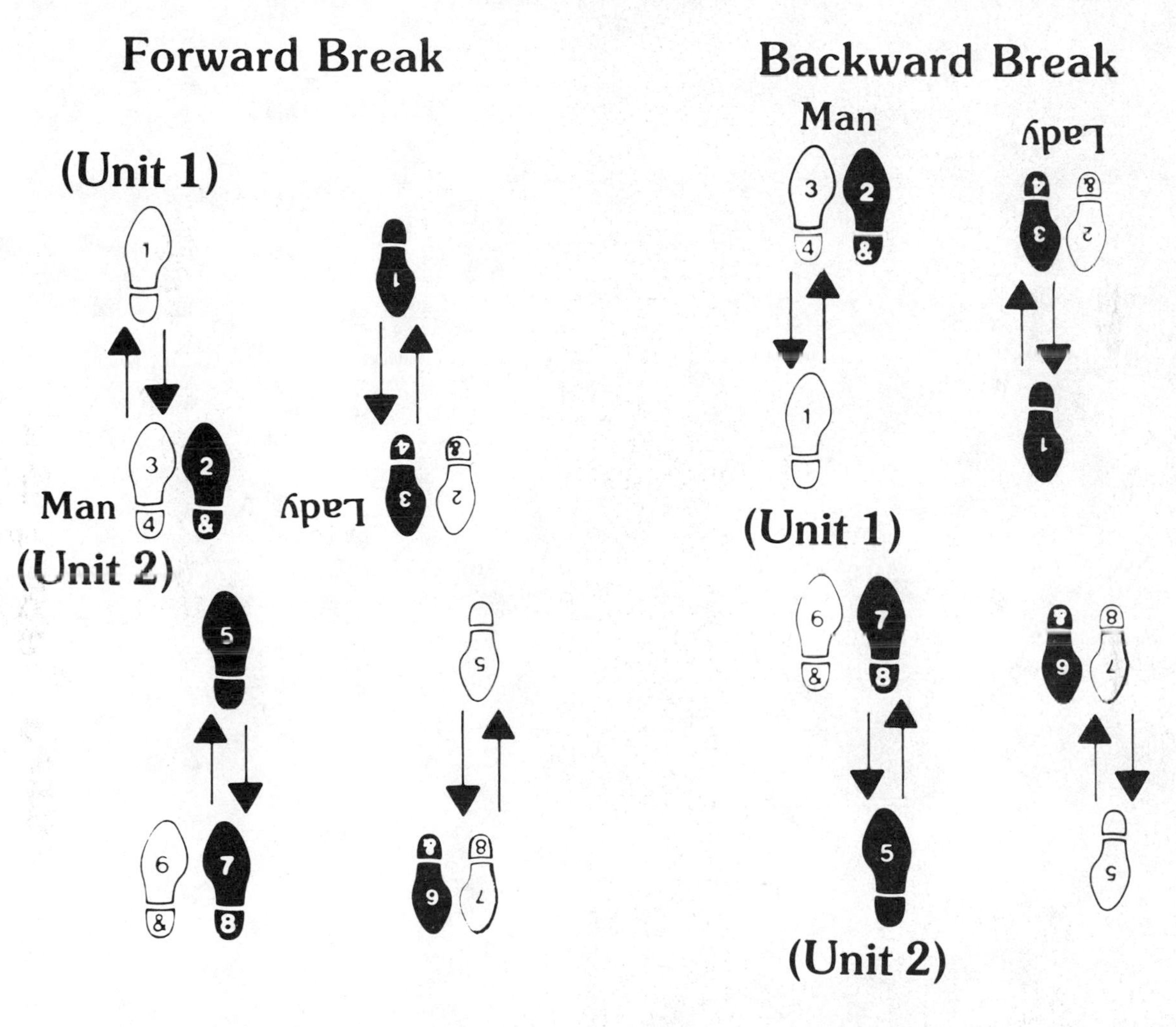

Step	Position	Directions	Hand Lead
Backward Basic	Closed	B F cl ch Ch F B cl ch Ch	Palm, Elbow Elbow, Palm
Forward Break	Closed	F B cl ch Ch F B cl ch Ch	Elbow, Palm Elbow, Palm
Backward Break	Closed	B F cl ch Ch B F cl ch Ch	Palm Elbow Palm, Elbow

Sideward Steps

Step	Position	Directions	Hand Lead
Forward Sideward	Two Hand	F B sd cl Sd	Elbow, Palm, Palm
		B F sd cl Sd	Palm, Elbow
Backward Sideward	Two Hand	B F sd cl Sd	Palm, Elbow, Palm
		F B sd cl Sd	Elbow, Palm

Forward

Backward

Lady

Lady

Man

Man

Forward and Sideward

Unit 1. Man raises his right elbow and steps forward on his left foot (slow), back on his right foot (slow), and sideward on his left foot (quick), closes right to left (quick), and steps sideward on his left foot (slow).
Unit 2. Man presses palm of right hand on lady's back and steps on his right foot (slow), forward on his left foot (slow), sideward on his right foot (quick), closes left to right (quick), and steps sideward right (slow).
Lady dances counterpart.

Backward and Sideward

Unit 1. Man presses with palm of right hand and steps back on his left foot (slow), sideward on his left foot (quick), closes right to left foot (quick), and steps sideward right (slow).
Unit 2. Man steps forward on his right foot (slow), back on his left foot (slow), and sideward on his right (quick), closes left to right (quick), and steps sideward on his right foot (slow).

Sideward Rock Step

Unit 1. The man steps side left (slow), then side right (slow), and marks time in place, L R L (quick quick slow).
Unit 2. The man steps side right (slow), side left (slow), then marks time in place, R L R (quick quick slow). The lady dances the same footwork, starting on the right foot.

Step	Position	Directions	Hand Lead
Sideward Rock	Conversation	Sd Sd cl ch Ch Sd Sd cl ch Ch	Palm Palm

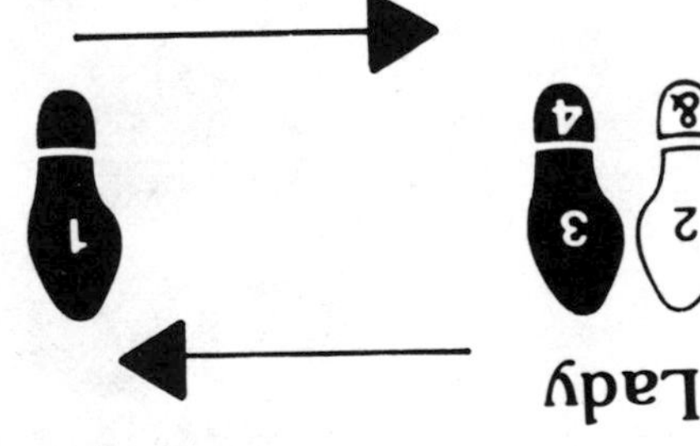

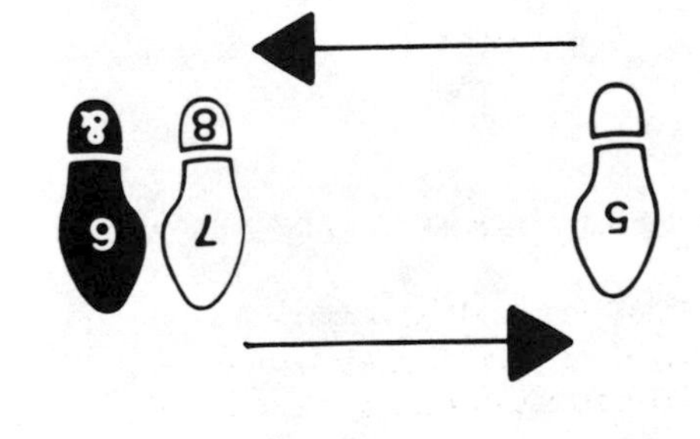

Lady

Man

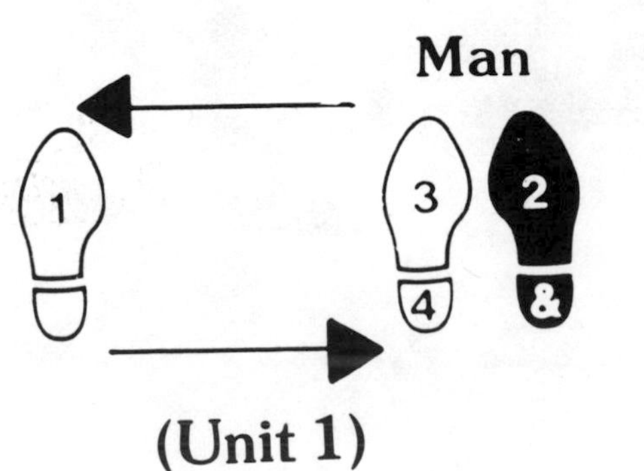

(Unit 1)

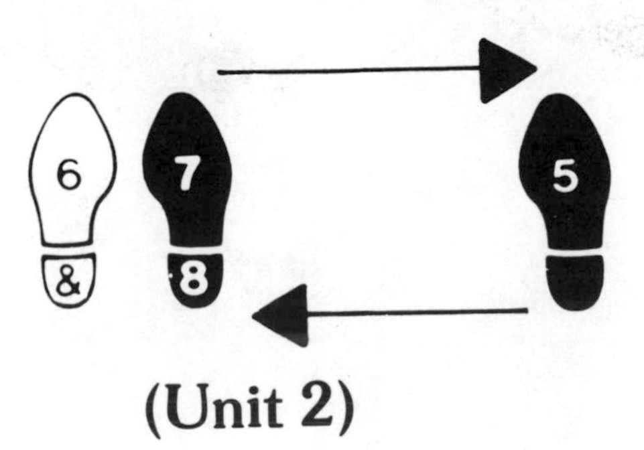

(Unit 2)

Turning Steps

Right Rock Turn (Closed Position)

Unit 1. Man steps back on left foot (slow) and turns one-quarter right. Then he steps forward on right foot, closes left foot to right foot, and marks time in place, L R L (quick quick slow).
Unit 2. Man steps forward on right foot (slow) as he turns one-quarter right. Rock on left foot (slow), then close right to left and mark time in place, R L R (quick quick slow). Lady dances opposite footwork, starting on right foot.

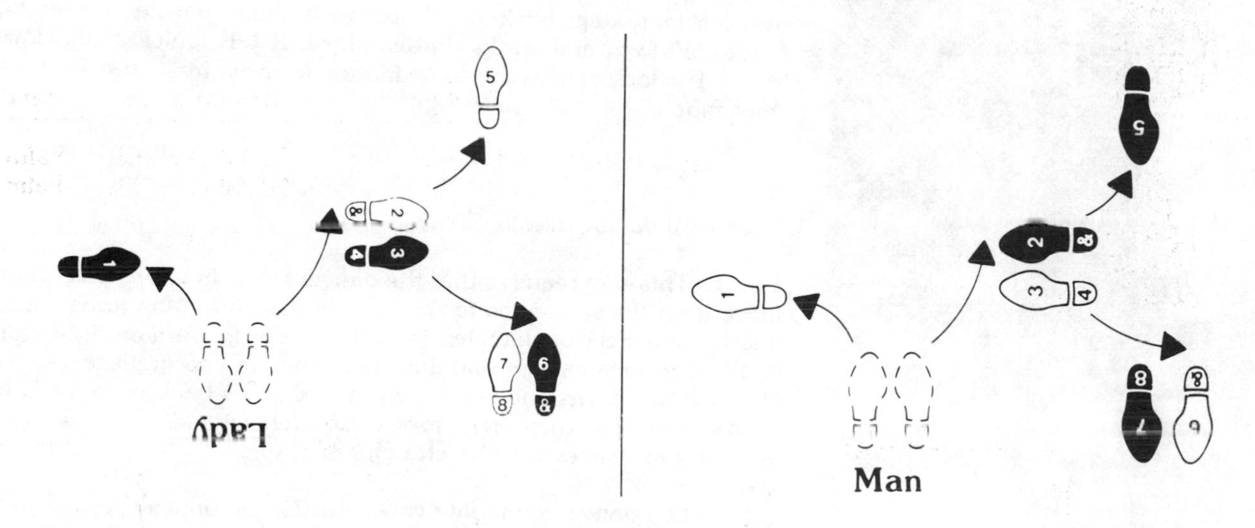

Left Rock Turn (Closed Position)

Unit 1. Man turns left and steps forward on left foot (slow) and back on right foot (slow), closes left to right, and marks time, L R L (quick quick slow).
Unit 2. Man turns one-quarter left and steps back on right foot (slow). Close right to left and mark time on the spot, R L R (quick quick slow). Lady opposite footwork, starting on right foot.

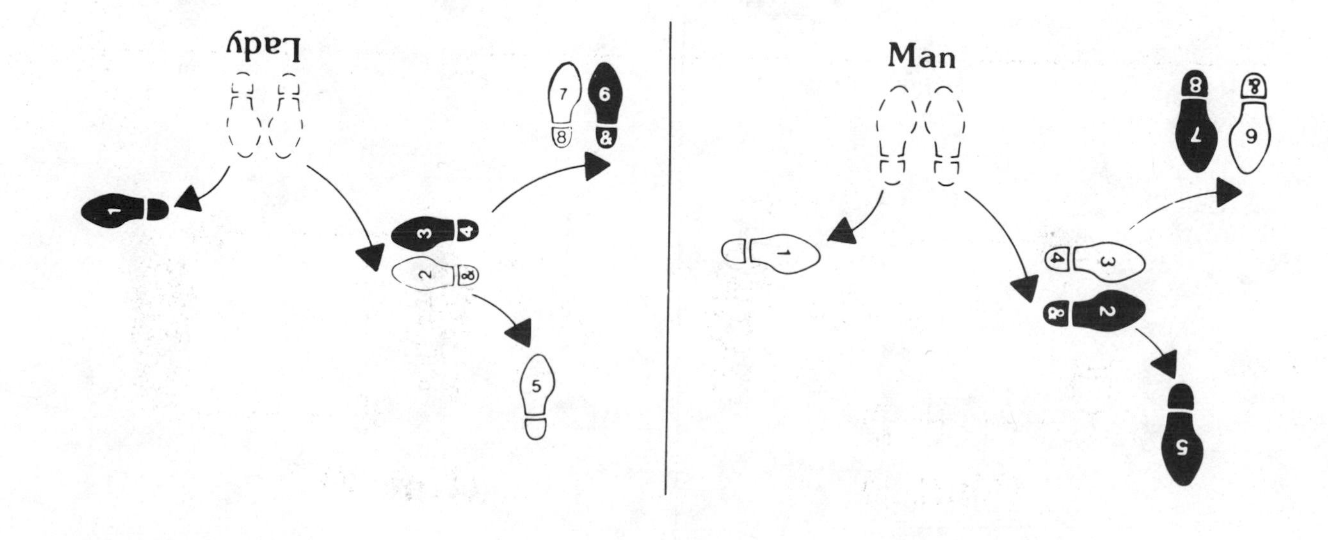

Changing Positions

Unit 1. Start in closed position and move to reverse then semi-open positions. Man turns right one-quarter and crosses left foot over right foot, then steps back on right foot as he truns to face partner. He closes left foot to right foot and marks time in place, L, R, L, (quick, quick, slow).

Unit 2. Man gives lead with heel of right hand and crosses right foot over left foot, steps back on left foot as he faces partner, closes right foot to left foot, and marks time in place, R L R (quick quick slow).

The lady dances the same footwork throughout, starting on the right foot.

Backward Junior Break

Unit 1. This step requires that the dancers start in closed position and move from the semi-open to the reverse position. Man turns left one-quarter and steps back on left foot, then steps forward on right foot as he turns to face partner and does the cha cha cha in place.
Unit 2. Man turns one-quarter right and steps back on right foot in reverse position, then steps forward on left foot as he turns to face partner and dances the cha cha cha in place.

Lady dances same footwork, starting on opposite foot

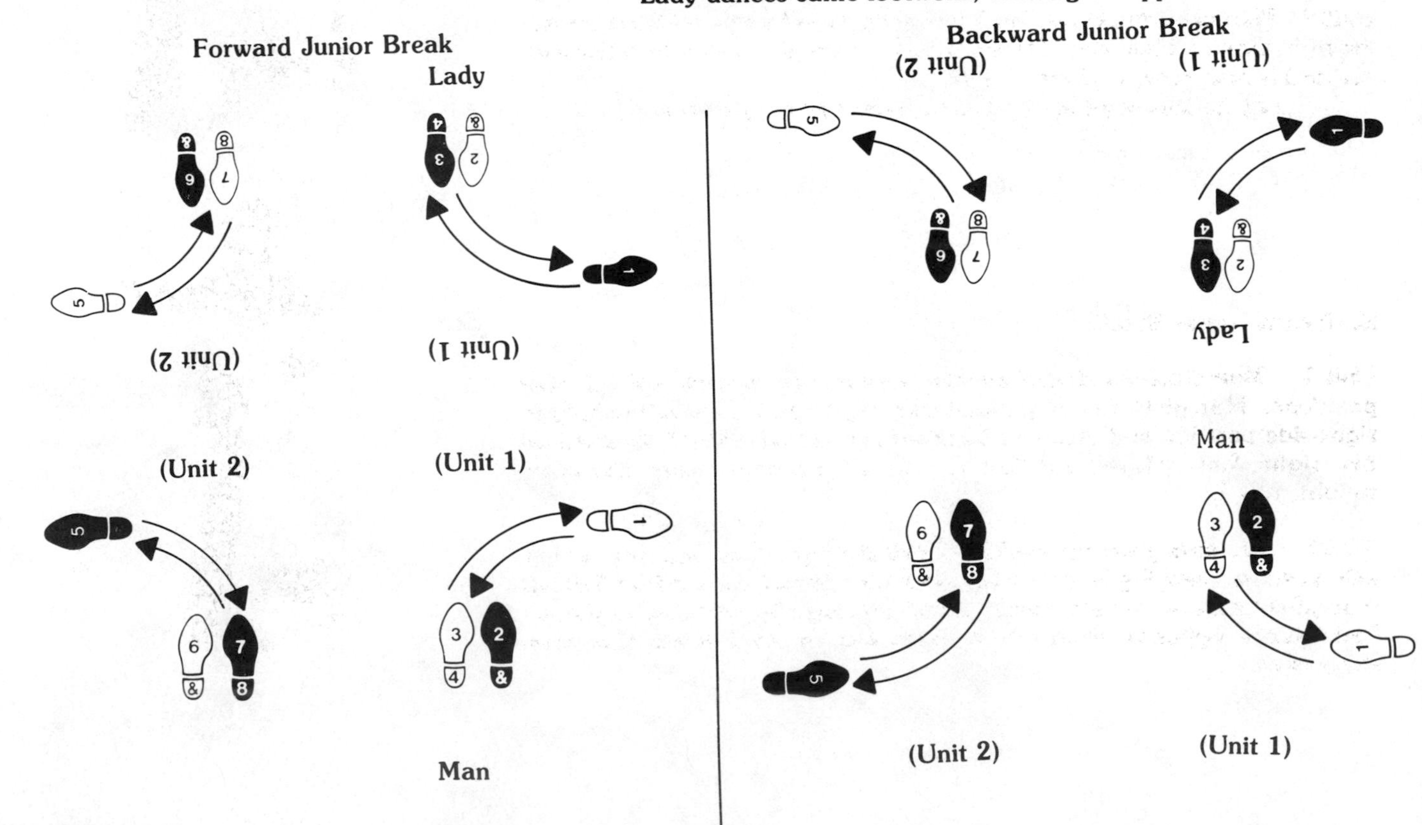

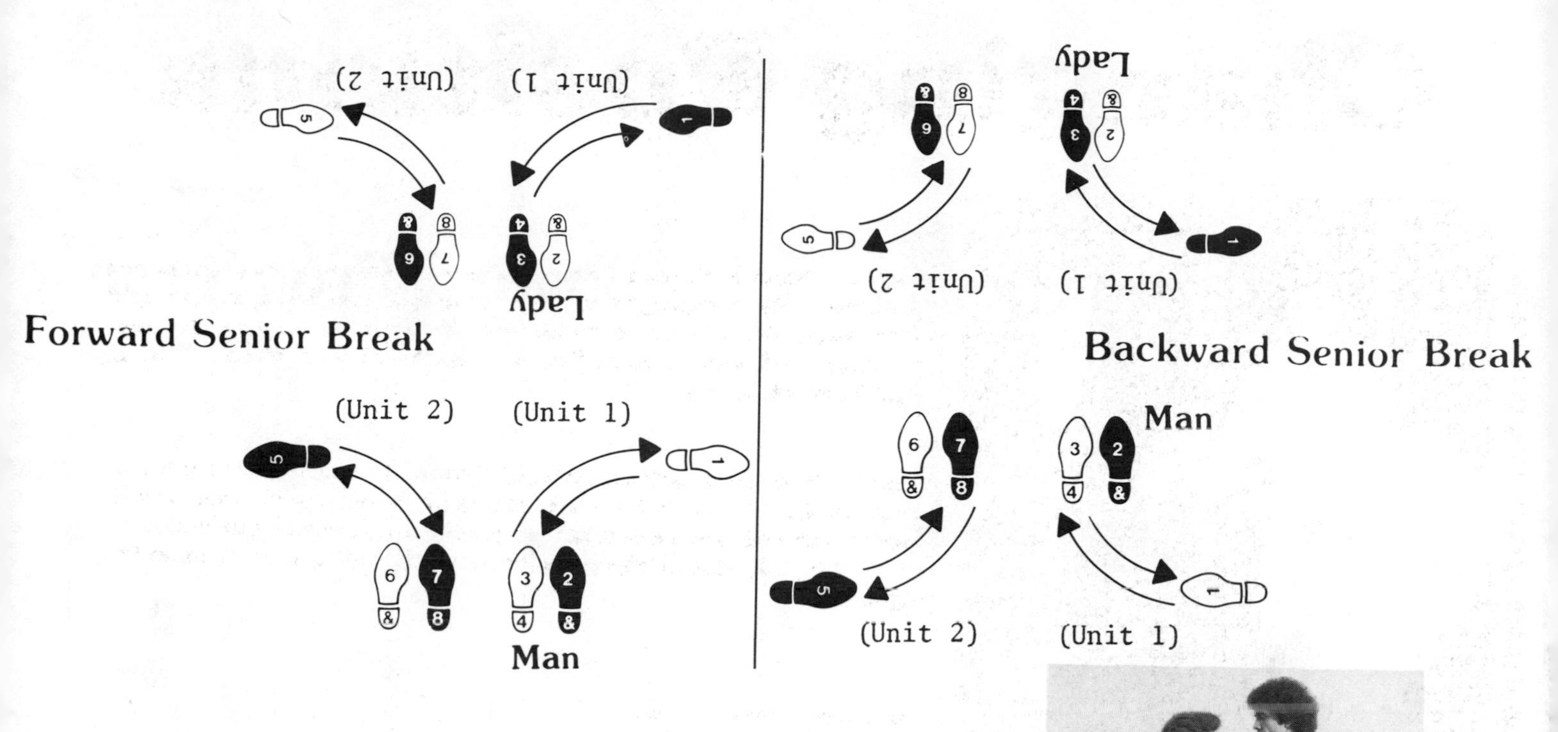

Forward Senior Break

Unit 1. This step requires that the dancers start in closed position and move to left- and right-side positions. Man gives a heel lead and turns to left-side position as he steps forward on left foot, then he steps back on his right foot as he turns to face his partner for the cha cha cha steps.
Unit 2. Man gives the finger lead and turns to right-side position, crossing right foot over left foot. He steps back on his left foot to face his partner and marks time in place, R L R.

Lady dances opposite footwork, starting on right foot.

Backward Senior Break

Unit 1. Man starts in closed position and moves to right and left side positions. Man gives the finger lead with right hand, turning the lady to right-side position and stepping back on his left foot (slow), forward on his right foot (slow), turning to closed position, and changing weight, L R L

Unit 2. The man gives the heel lead with the right hand and turns to left side postion, stepping back on his right foot (slow), forward on his left foot (slow),turning to face partner, and dancing cha cha cha in place. Lady starts opposite footwork by stepping forward when the man steps back.

Progressive Steps

Forward Progressive

Backward Progressive

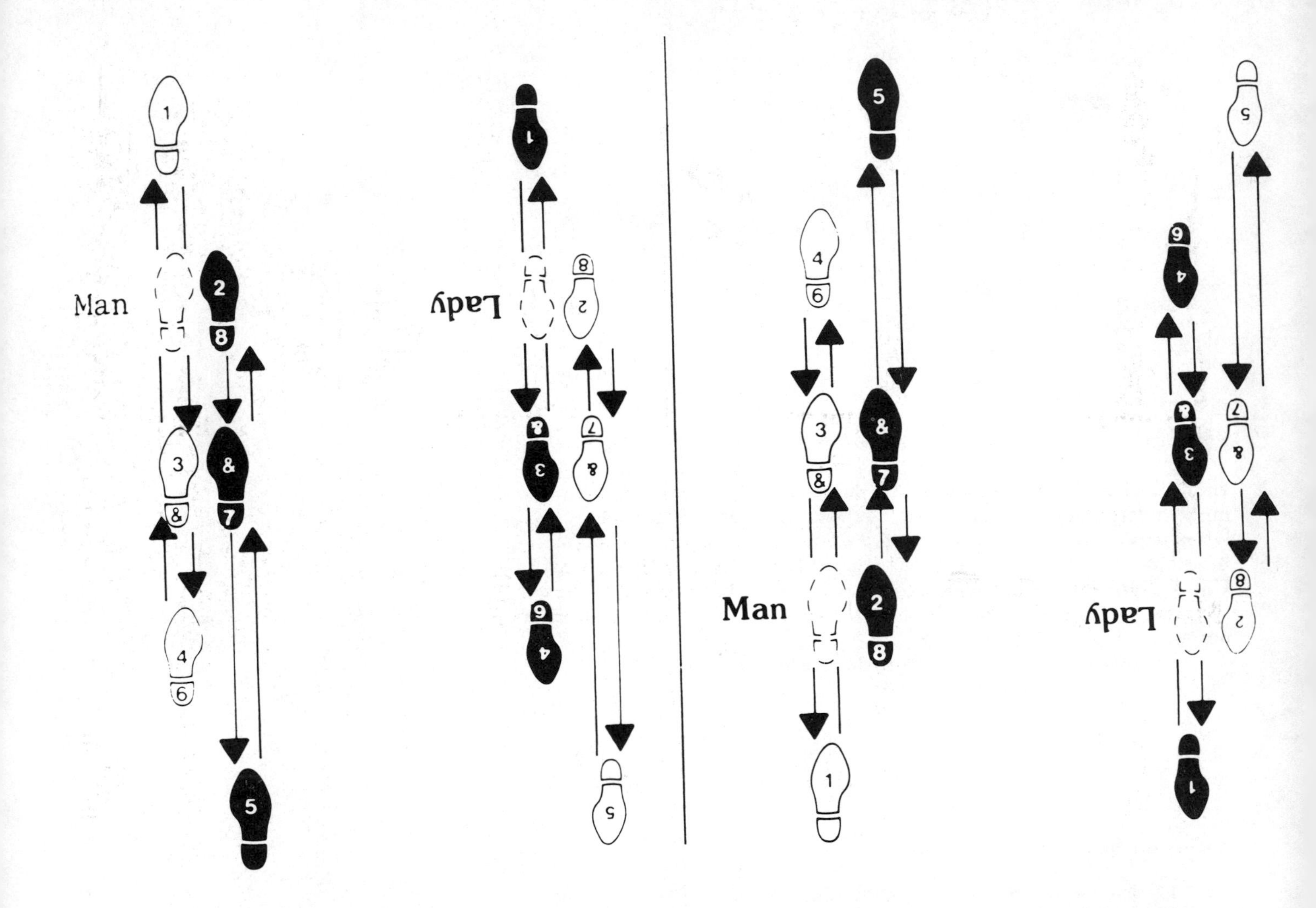

Step	Position	Directions	Hand Lead
Forward Progressive	Closed	F B b cl B B F f cl F	Elbow, Palm Palm, Elbow
Backward Progressive	Closed	B F f cl F F B b cl B	Palm, Elbow Elbow, Palm

Arching In and Out

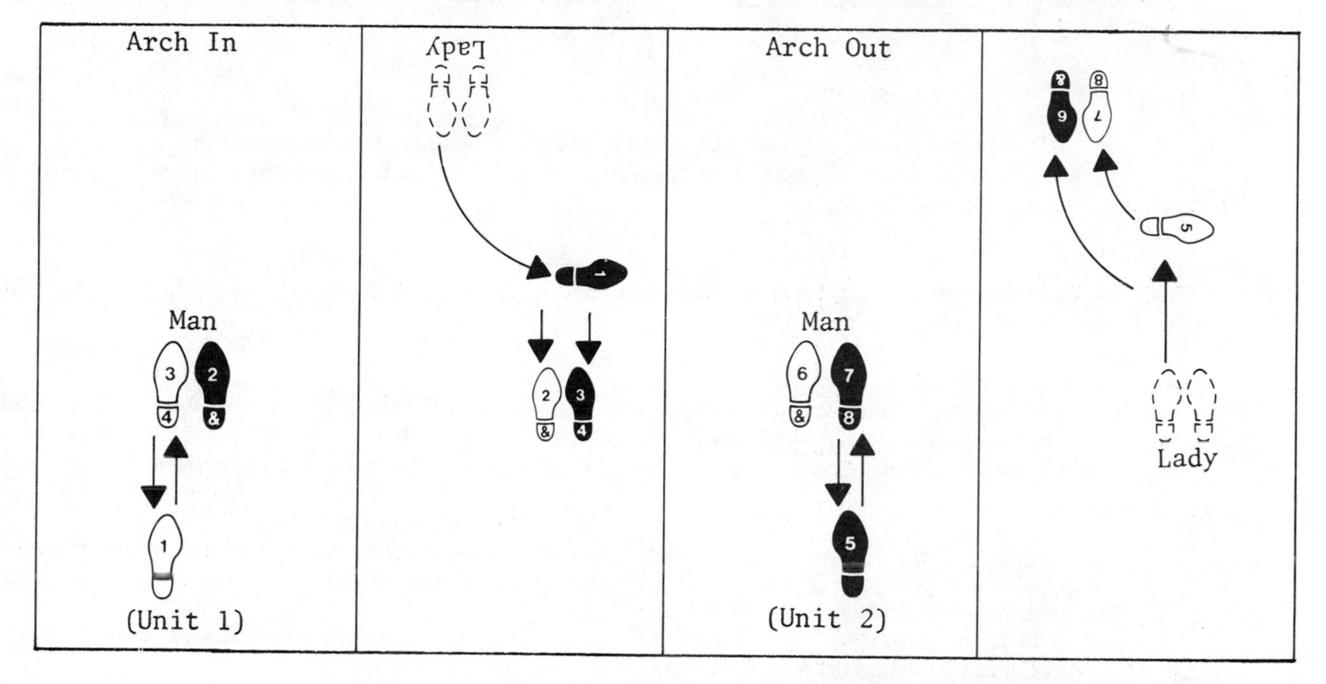

Arch In
Start in two-hand position. Man crosses his left hand high. Man dances the back break while the lady walks under arch into semi-open position.

Arch Out
Man raises his left hand high and dances the backward break. As the lady walks under, they arch to two-hand position.

RUMBA

The rumba is Cuban in origin and has probably the most pronounced rhythm of any dance that we dance today. Rumba is the most popular of all Latin American dances and was the first dance from south of the border to interest North Americans

Rhythm
Rumba music is technically 2/4 in rhythm but for dance purposes is considered 4/4 with four beats to the measure, one slow and two quick movements.

Tempo
Slow rumba is 120 to 150 quarter notes to the minute, basic rumba is danced to this tempo. 150 to 200 is medium, and combinations of break rhythms and basic are danced to this tempo; 200 and over is fast, and break rhythm is danced to this tempo. The slow and medium tempos are best for ballroom dancing.

Style
The chief difference between the rumba and the two-step is in the style. The more important styles of rumba are Cuban-American, Cuban, and Puerto Rican. Of these, the Puerto Rican is the most smoothly styled and, therefore, the most desirable for ballroom dancing.

American Rumba takes the weight on each step; however, the same movement and style should be applied as in the Cuban and Puerto Rican Rumba.

In the Cuban Rumba, you move your foot then change weight. In the American Rumba, you shift your weight as you move your feet.

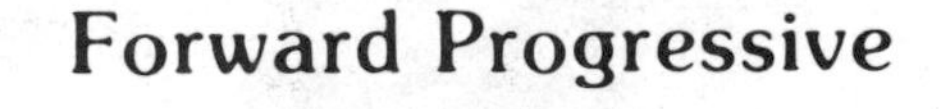

4 & 3
1 & 2
man

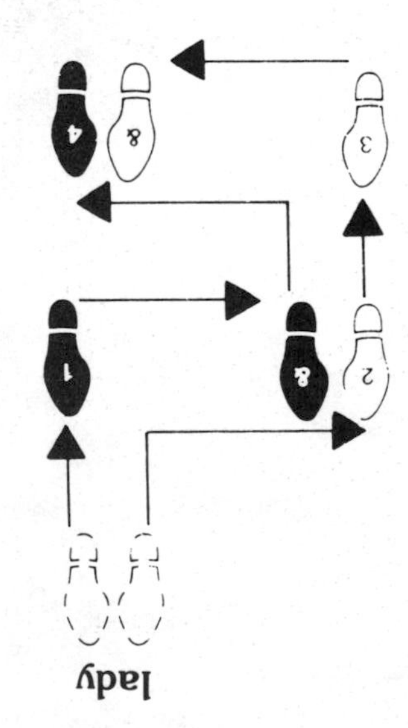

Backward Progressive

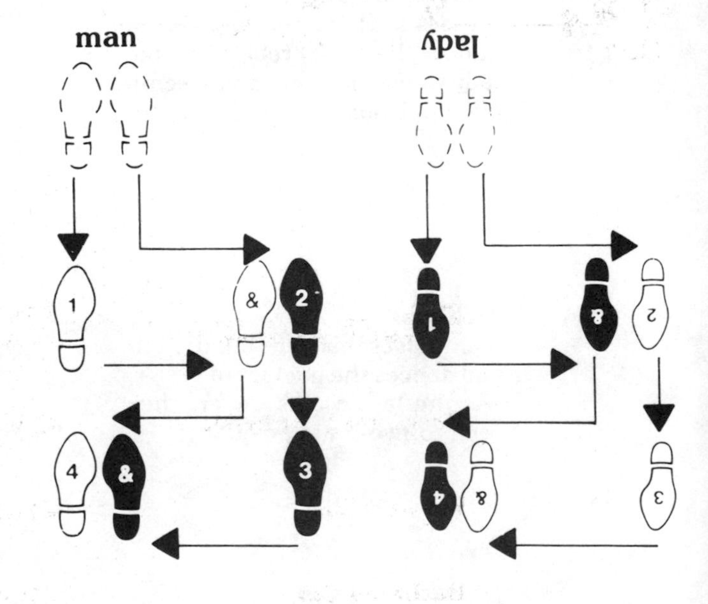

Forward Progressive (Closed Position)
This is the same step as the backward step in the box rhythm foxtrot. The forward progressive step in the rumba is also the same as in the waltz box except that the dance rhythm is "SLOW quick quick" and the style is Latin rather than American.

Backward Progressive (Closed Position)
This step is the same as the backward progressive in the box rhythm of the foxtrot.

Forward Box (Closed Position)
This is the same as the forward box in the box rhythm of the foxtrot. However, the style is emphasizing a delayed action on each step.

Backward Box (Closed Postition)
This foot pattern is the same as the backward box step in the box rhythm of the foxtrot. The difference is in the style of the dance.

Forward Box

Backward Box

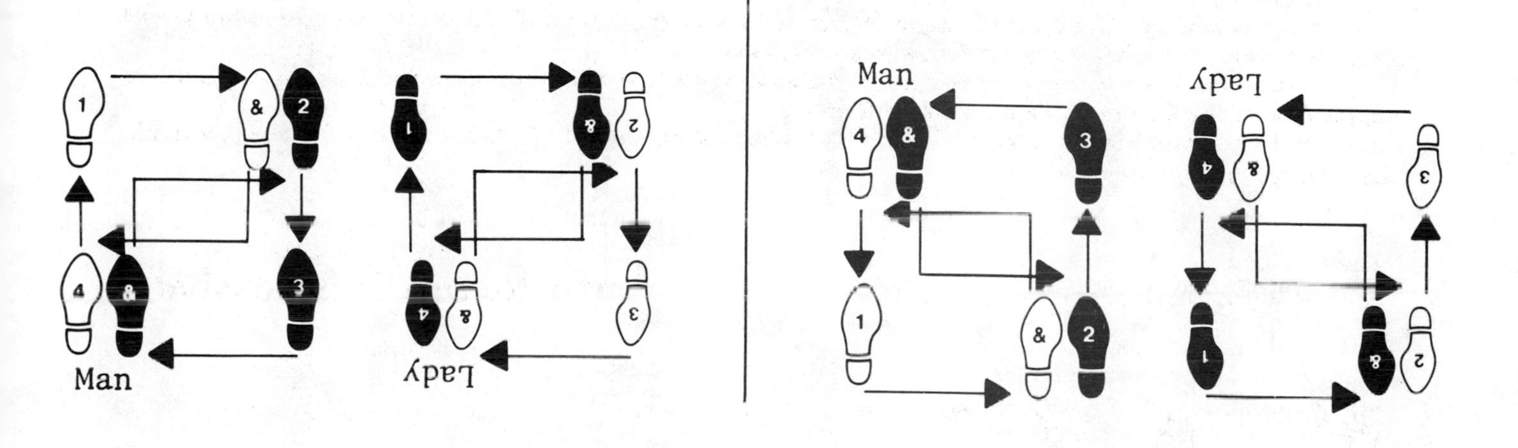

Step	Position	Directions	Hand Lead
Forward Progressive	Closed	F sd cl-F sd cl	Elbow, Palm Elbow, Palm
Backward Progressive	Closed	B sd cl-B sd cl	Palm, Palm Palm, Palm
Forward Box	Closed	F sd cl-B sd cl	Elbow, Palm Palm, Palm
Backward Box	Closed	B sd cl-F sd cl	Palm, Palm Elbow, Palm

The Cuban walk rhythm is done either forward or backward without bringing the feet together. The Latin motion, famous as well as essential, comes from bending then straightening the knee. To get the proper knee motion, try walking up a flight of stairs very slowly, concentrating on the "natural action" of the knee. It is important that the step taken by squeezing the inside of the foot and rolling the weight to the flat of the foot. The weight should shift past the center flat of the foot. The squeezing of the weight from the inside of the foot to the flat is done smoothly and is synchronized with the motion of the knees. This basic motion is used in the majority of Latin dancing.

Forward Walk

&, 4, 3, &, 2, 1

man

&, 4, 3, &, 2, 1

lady

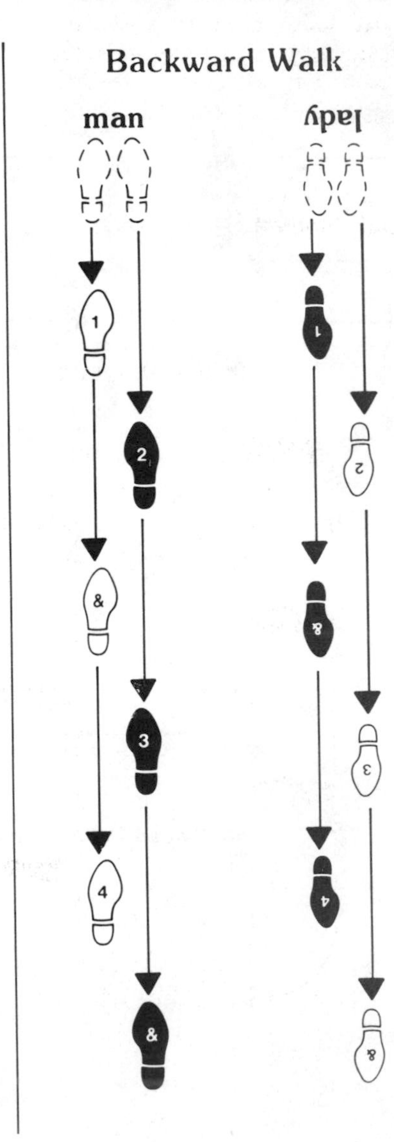

Sideward Steps

Forward Walk (Closed Position)
This step is like the forward walk in the collegiate walk foxtrot rhythm, except that this rhythm is "slow quick quick" and the style is Latin.

Backward Walk (Closed Position)
The foot pattern and lead are the same as in the backward walk in the collegiate walk foxtrot rhythm.

Front Cross (Conversation Position)
The heel lead is used to get the lady to cross forward. Man steps sideward and back with left foot, then crosses right foot in front of left foot.

Lady does the opposite footwork.

Front Cross

Back Cross

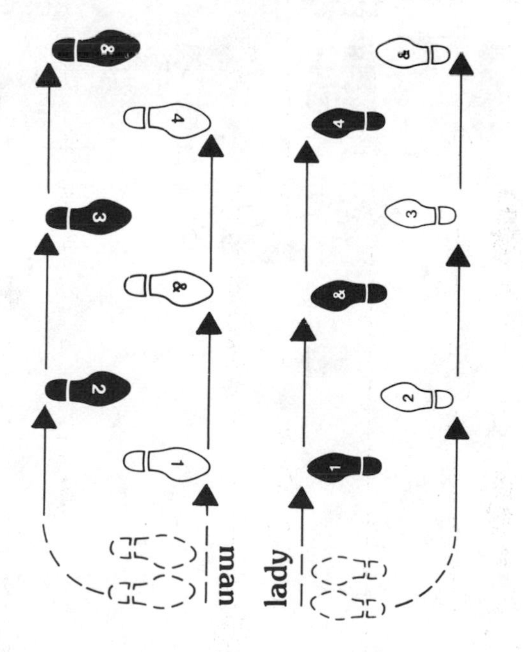

Back Cross (Conversation Position)
The man steps forward with left foot and crosses right behind left. The finger lead is used to get the lady to cross back and to do the same footwork as the man.

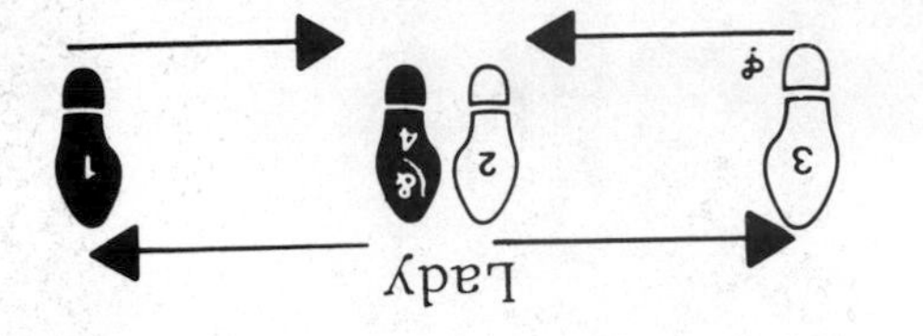

Sideward Basic Break (Conversation Position)

First Unit. Man steps sideward left (slow), then shifts weight sideward right (quick) and sideward left (quick), closing feet left to right. Lady dances the same footwork starting on opposite foot.
Second Unit. Man steps to the side with the right foot (slow), to the side with left foot (quick), and closes right to left (quick).

Man

Turning Steps

Right Box Turn

Left Box Turn

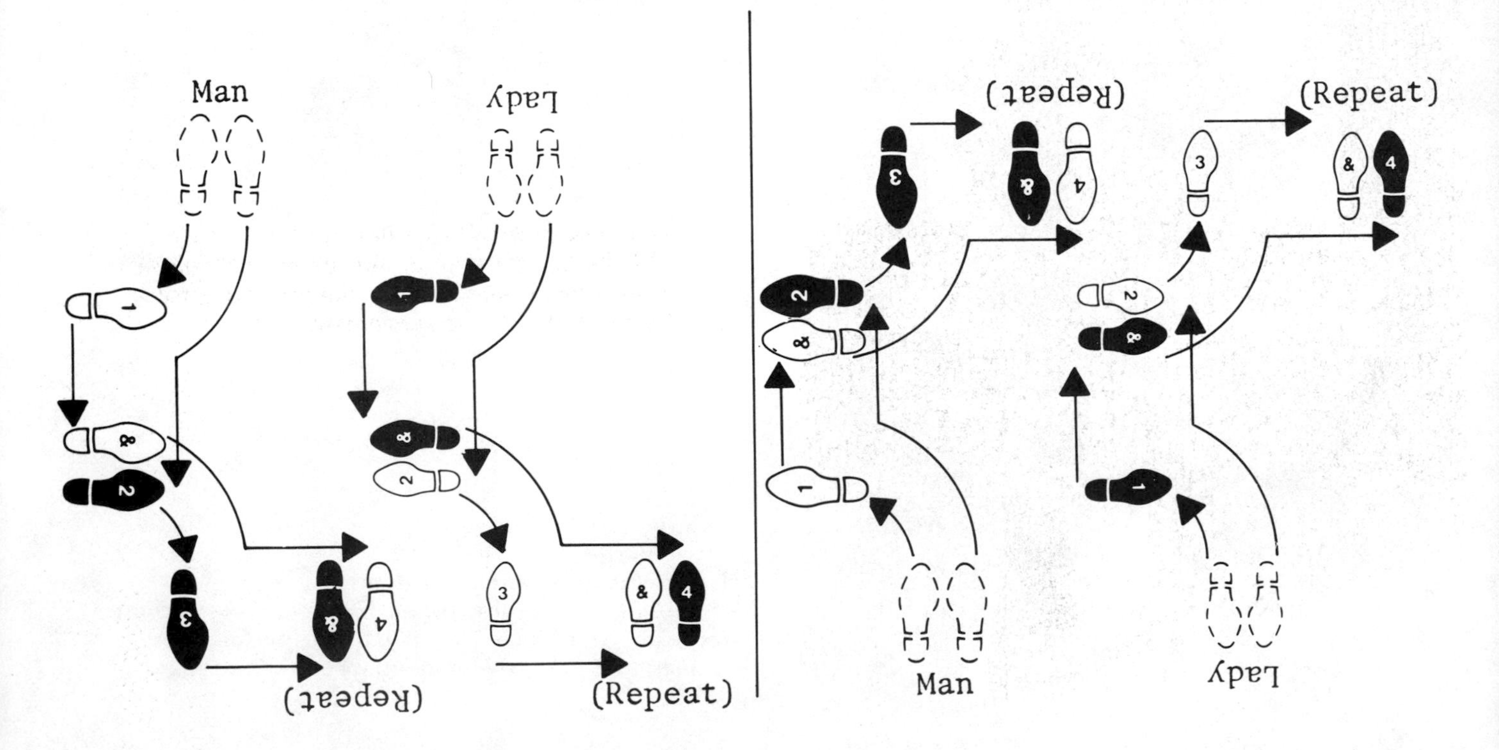

Right Box Turn (Closed Position)
This foot pattern is danced exactly like the right turn in the box rhythm of the foxtrot using the Cuban style. Lady dances counterpart.

Left Box Turn (Closed Position)
This foot pattern is like the left box turn in the foxtrot box rhythm. Lady dances counterpart using the Latin hip movement.

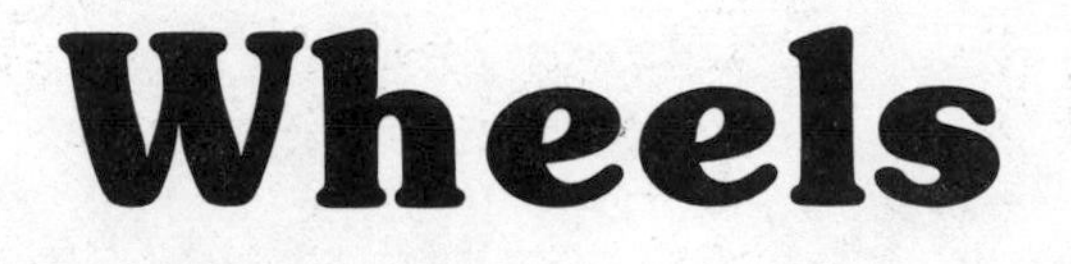

Forward Right-Side Wheel

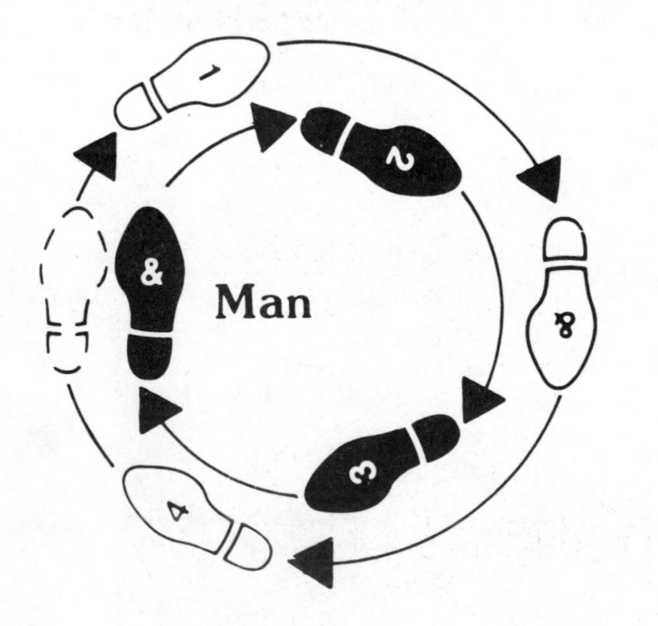

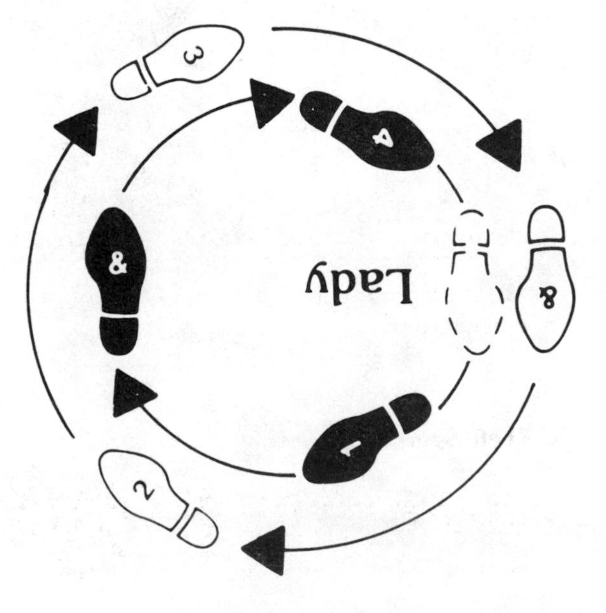

Right Spot Pivot

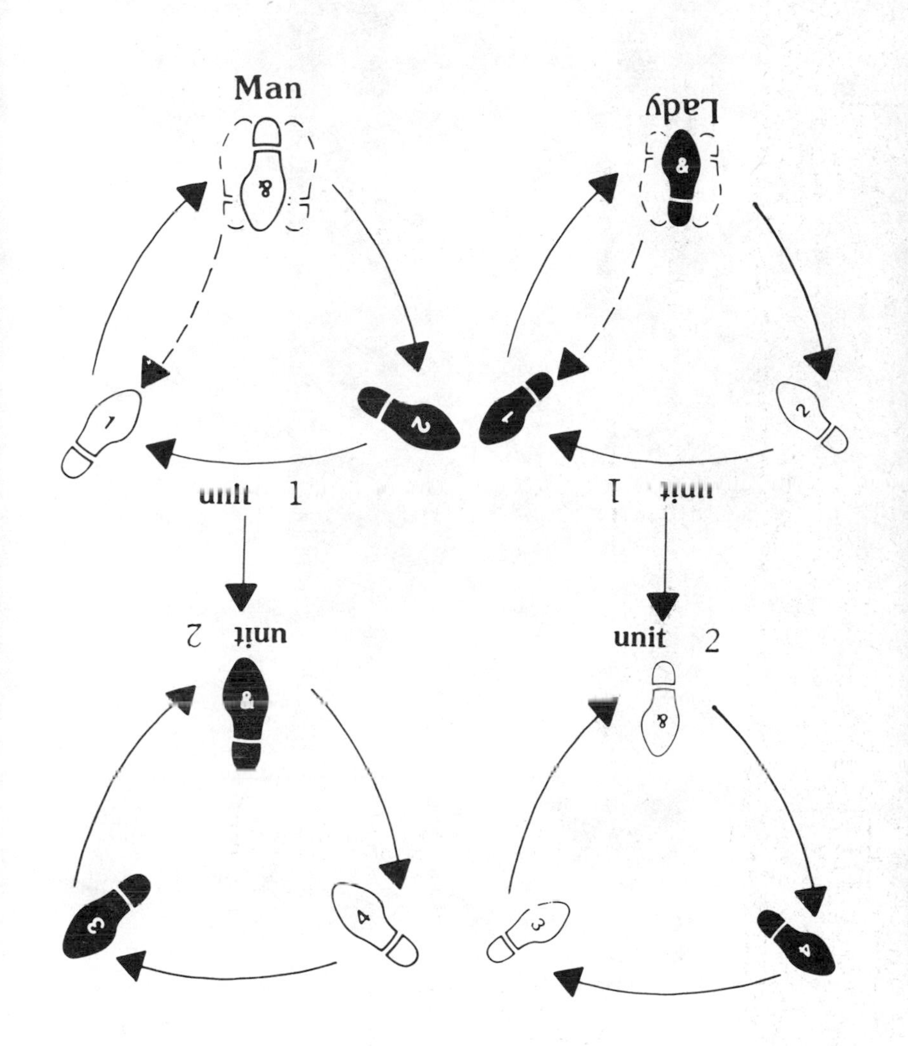

Step	Position	Directions	Hand Lead
Right Spot Pivot	Closed	B f b / (tr ½)	Heel
		F b f / (tr ½)	Heel
Left Spot Pivot	Closed	F b f / (tl ½)	Fingers
		B f b / (tl ½)	Fingers

SAMBA

The samba is particularly appealing to young people but has become very popular with dancers of all ages. It first appeared in American ballrooms with a very bouncy style, but it since has been modified and is now a delightfully gay dance with an intriguing rhythm.

Rhythm
Samba rhythm is unique in that the accent falls on the second beat of a 2/4 measure. Four measures usually are played to each phrase, and the dance step patterns should fall into this same phrasing. Rhythm is quick quick slow.

Tempo
A quarter-note count of 110 or fewer to the minute is considered slow samba; 110 or 130 counts is medium; and 130 and over is fast samba.

Style
The exaggerated bounce of the early samba is now obsolete. The best style of today gives it a smooth, lilting movement. A well-toned relaxation in the knees and ankles permits one to execute the steps with little exertion yet get the full satisfaction that this youthful dance has to offer. The head is held still as the body moves forward and backward and sideward, like a swing pendulum. To perform the rocking movement of the samba step, keep the knees bent on count 1 and straighten them on count 2.

Forward Basics

Man

Lady

Forward Pendulum

Step	Position	Direction	Hand Lead
Forward Basic	Closed	f cl Ch f cl Ch	Elbow Elbow
Forward Pendulum	Closed	f cl Ch b cl Ch	Elbow Palm

Man

Lady

Side Steps

Front Ball Change

Back Ball Change

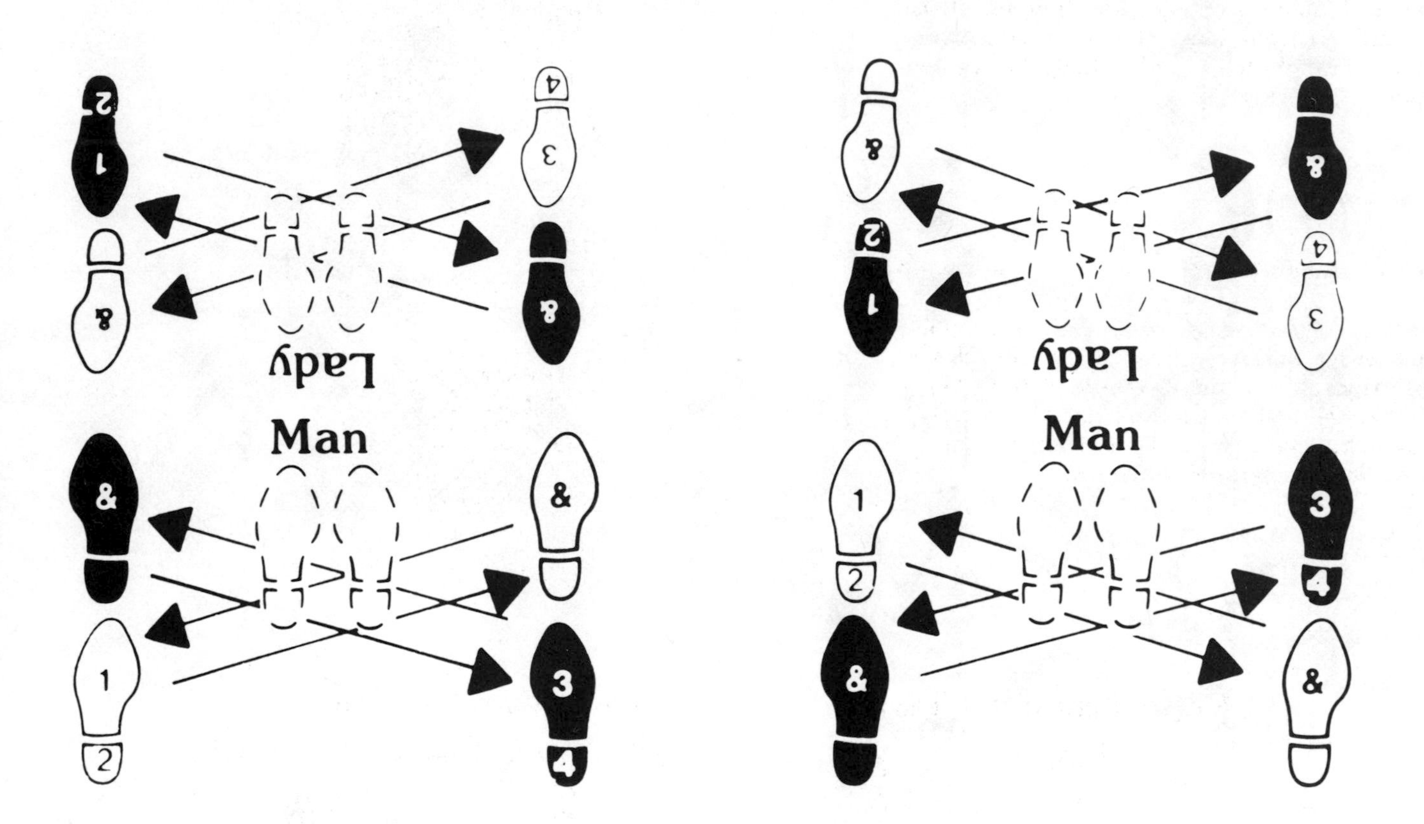

Front Ball Change

Unit 1. Man steps to side left foot. Cross right foot over left and change weight to right foot then to left.
Unit 2. Man steps right on right foot, crosses left in front of right and changes weight to left foot then right.

Back Ball Change (Conversation Position)

Unit 1. Man steps forward on left foot and closes right foot behind left changing weight.

Turns

Right Pendulum Turn (Closed Position)

Unit 1. Man gives heel lead to turn one-quarter left, steps back on left foot, closes right, and changes weight right to left.
Unit 2. Man turns one-quarter right and steps forward on right foot, closes left foot, and changes weight left to right. Lady dances opposite footwork.

Left Pendulum Turn

Unit 1. Man gives finger lead, turns one-quarter left and steps forward left foot, closes with right, and changes weight right to left.
Unit 2. Man steps back on right foot, closes with left, and changes weight left to right. Lady dances opposite footwork.

Right Pendulum Turn

Man

Lady

(Repeat)

Left Pendulum Turn

(Repeat)

Man

Lady

Forward Right-Side Wheel

Unit 1. Man gives palm lead and steps forward on left foot, closes right, and changes weight right to left.
Unit 2. Man steps forward right foot, closes with left foot, and changes weight left to right. Lady dances same footwork, starting on opposite foot.

Backward Right-Side Wheel

Unit 1. Man raises right elbow and steps back on left foot, closes right foot, and changes weight right to left.
Unit 2. Man steps back on right foot, closes left foot, and changes weight left to right.

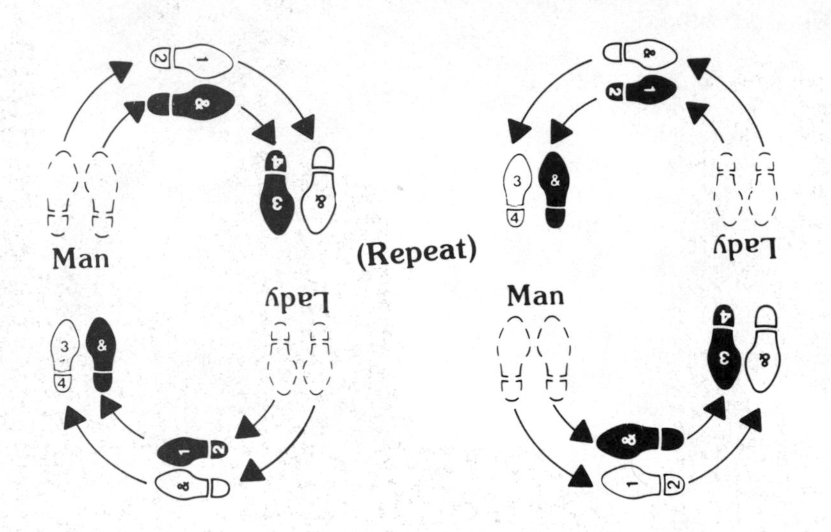

Forward Left-Side Wheel

Unit 1. Man gives palm lead and steps forward on left foot, closing right, and changes weight right to left.
Unit 2. Man steps forward on right foot, closes left, and changes weight left to right. Lady dances same footwork.

Backward Left-Side Wheel

Unit 1. Man raises right elbow and steps back with left foot, closes with right foot, and changes weight from right to left.
Unit 2. Man steps back on right foot, closes left, and changes weight from left to right. Lady dances same footwork, starting on opposite foot.

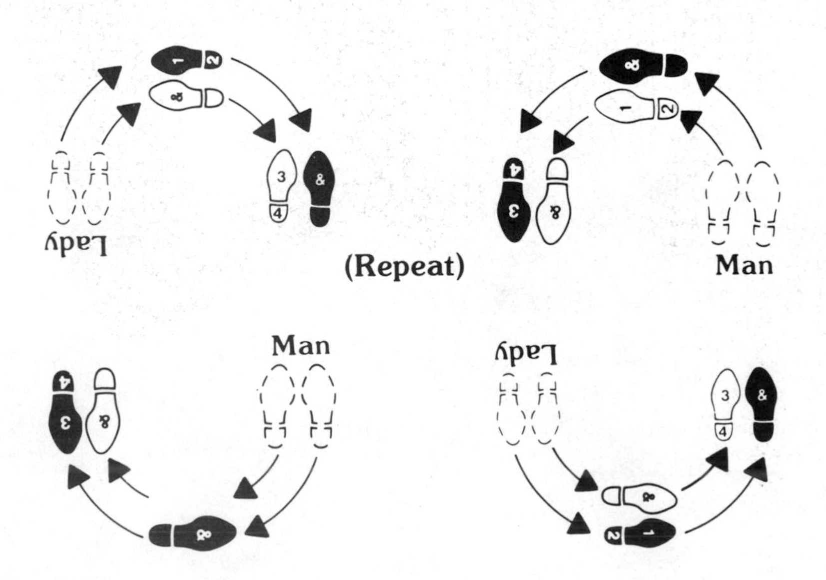

TANGO

The tango originated in Argentina as an intensely emotional dance often referred to as a "love dance." Over the years it developed a more refined yet invigorating style. Toward the beginning of the twentieth century the tango became popular as a ballroom dance; about 1912 it was introduced to the United States as an exhibition dance.

Since then it has remained a favorite of musicians and dancers alike. Because of its stimulating music, ease of execution, adaptability to crowded floors, and expressive style, the tango is considered an ideal--possibly the ideal--ballroom dance. Frequently called the "dancer's dance," it is the most highly styled of all classical ballroom dances. Trained dancers find great enjoyment in dancing the tango, and only experienced dancers can do it justice.

Rhythm
As it is currently played, the tango has four well-defined beats in each measure. Frequently the first beat is preceded by a slur. For teaching pruposes, each basic step is completed in one measure.

Argentine Tango has a basic rhythm of "slow, slow, quick, quick, draw," counted as one measure of music to complete one basic step.

Tempo
The tempo has an average of 126 quarter-note counts per minute.

Style
Give special attention to the line of balance and keep all dances characterized by frequent dips, bent knees, and catlike movements.

For teaching purposes each step is considered as one measure. No weight is taken on the fourth count. Hold, touch, and draw indicate no transfer of weight.

Dancers should take long steps with a slight bend of the knee. Dancers should dance with their bodies slightly closer than in other dances, using contra-body movements with smooth staccato movements and reaching from the hips.

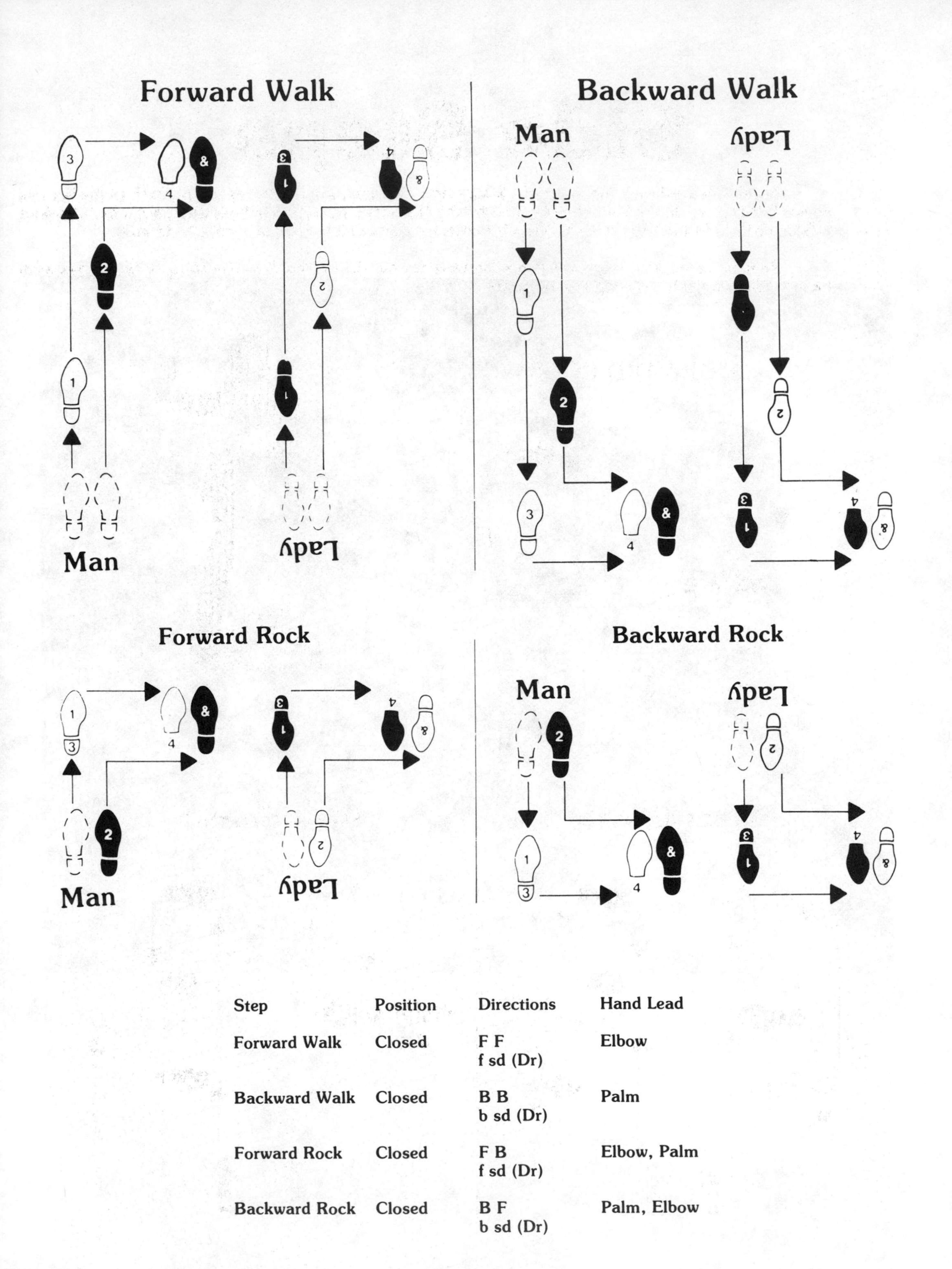

Step	Position	Directions	Hand Lead
Forward Walk	Closed	F F f sd (Dr)	Elbow
Backward Walk	Closed	B B b sd (Dr)	Palm
Forward Rock	Closed	F B f sd (Dr)	Elbow, Palm
Backward Rock	Closed	B F b sd (Dr)	Palm, Elbow

Side Steps

In the sideward rock the man does a sideward rock unit, then shifts his weight back to the left and does a "side draw." In the front cross he does a front cross unit, then steps in front with his left foot and does a "side draw." In the back cross he does a backward cross unit instead of a front cross unit.

As in all other cross steps, the lady's footwork is opposite the man's but he can give her the opposite hand leads to have her do opposite footwork.

SIDEWARD ROCK

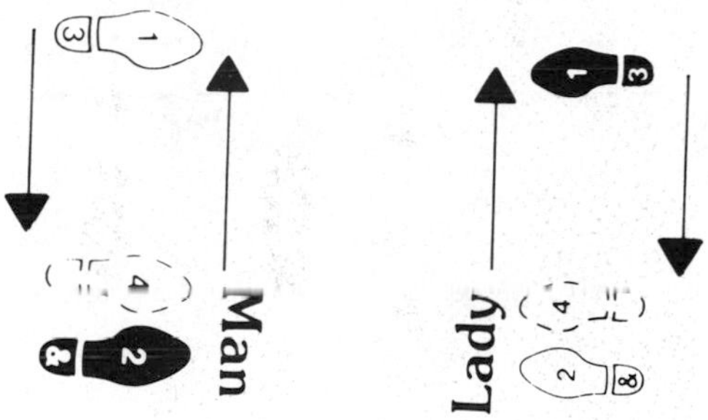

Front Cross

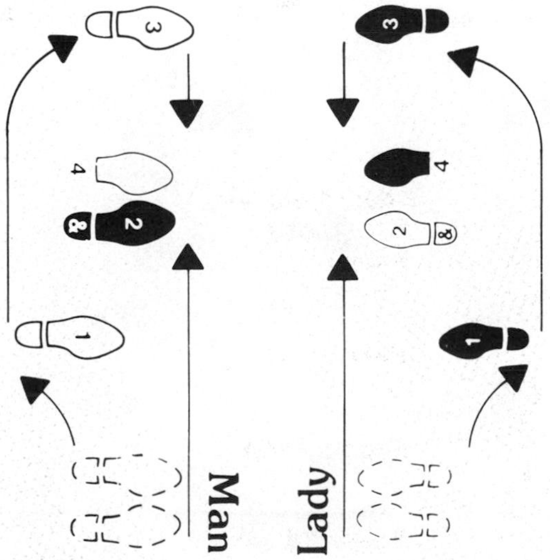

Back Cross

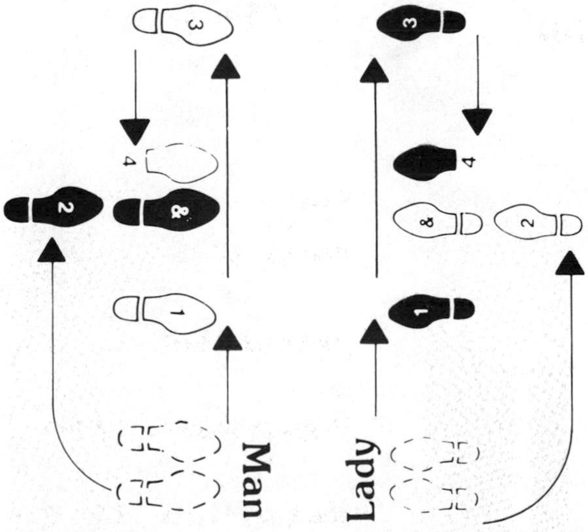

In the right rock turn the man turns right 1/4 turn on the first slow step of each backward rock unit or measure. In the left rock turn he turns left 1/4 turn on the first slow step of each forward rock unit. Because both partners turn only one-quarter of a turn per unit, a complete rock turn requires four measures.

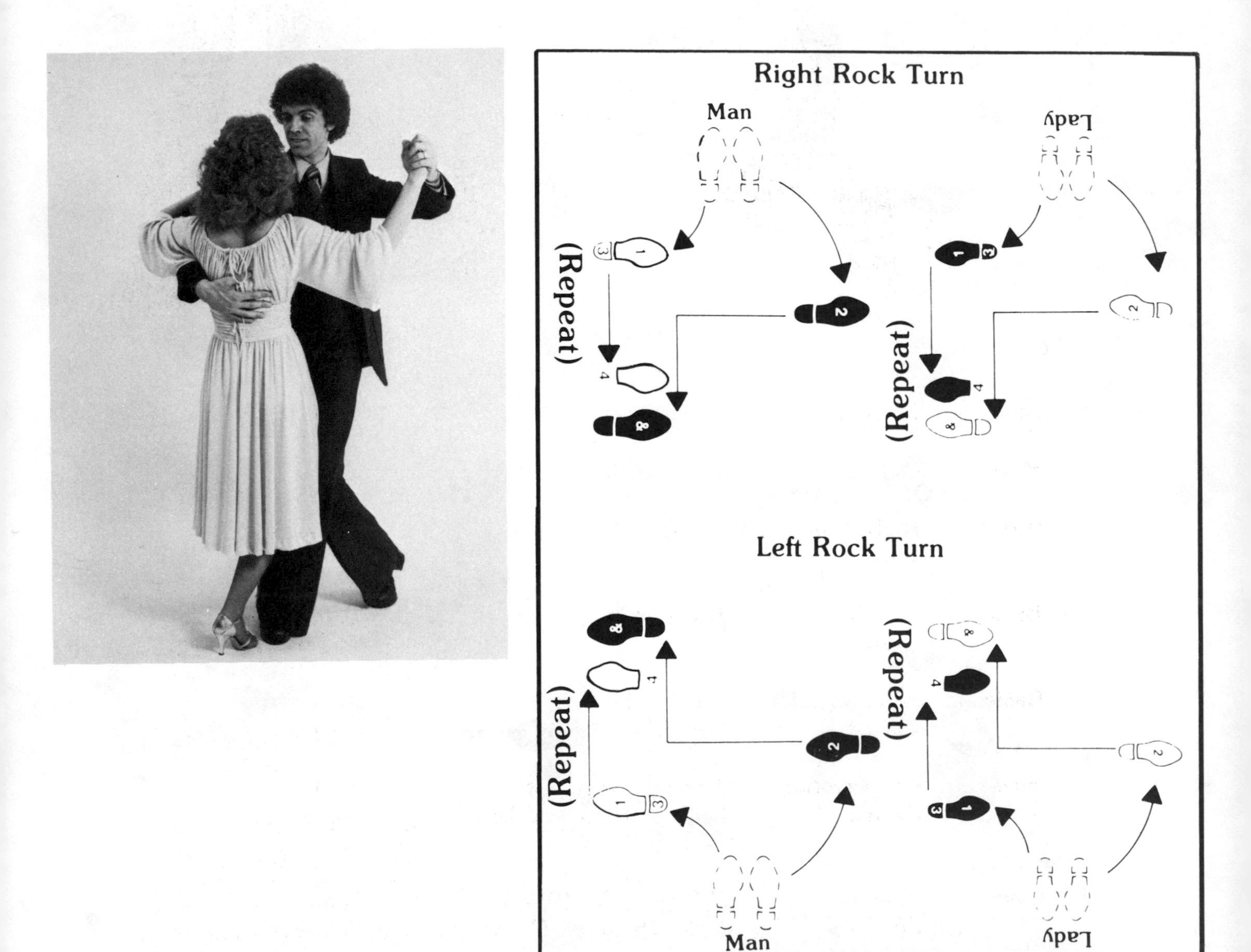

Step	Position	Directions	Hand Lead
Basic	Closed	F F f sd Dr	Elbow
Basic	Right Side Closed	F F f sd Dr	Elbow, Palm
Basic	Left Side Closed	B B <u>f</u> sd Dr {tl ½}	Palm, Palm Fingers
Basic	Semi-open Closed	F F f sd Dr Lady F F <u>b</u> sd Dr {tl ½	Palm *Fingers*
Basic	*Conversation* Closed	*SdX (F) f sd Dr* {tl ¼} Lady SdX (F) <u>b</u> sd Dr {tl ¼}	Heel fingers
Basic	*Reverse* *Closed*	*B B <u>sd</u> sd Dr* {tl ¼} *Lady B B <u>sd</u> sd Dr* {tr ¼}	*Palm* Fingers
Basic	Open Closed	F F f sd Dr Lady F F <u>b</u> sd Dr {tl ½}	Palm *Fingers*

Forward Arch	Closed Full-open	F F f sd Dr Lady F B b sd Dr {tr 1}	LH High Palm
Backward Arch	L Sd Full Open Closed	B B f sd Dr {tl ½} Lady B F b sd Dr {tl 1}	LH High Palm

Forward Arch

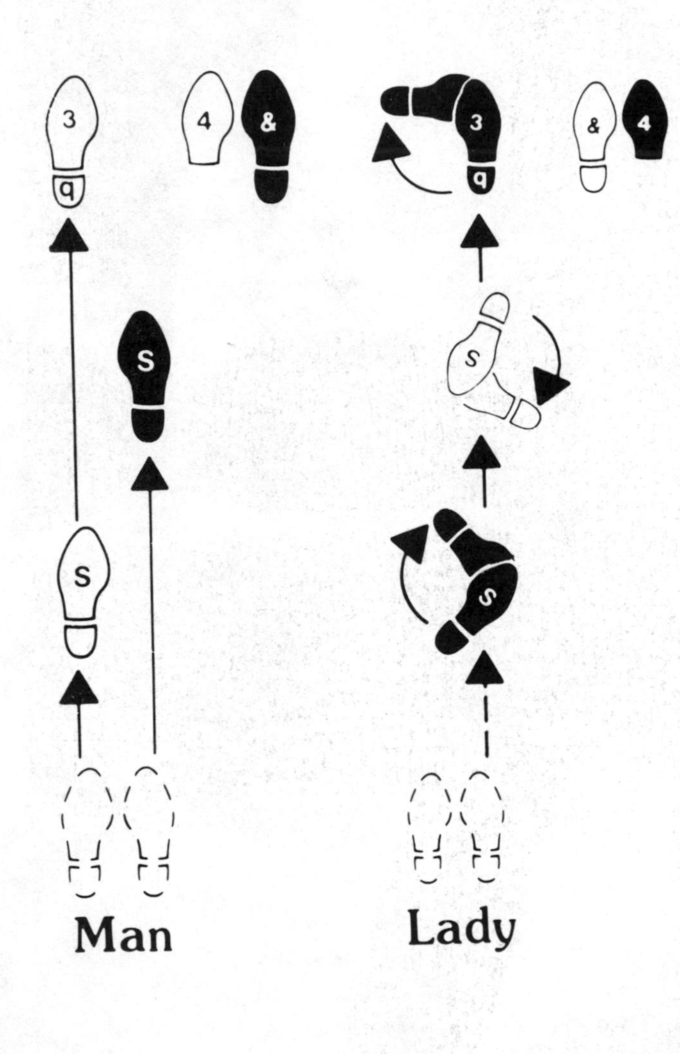

Backward Arch

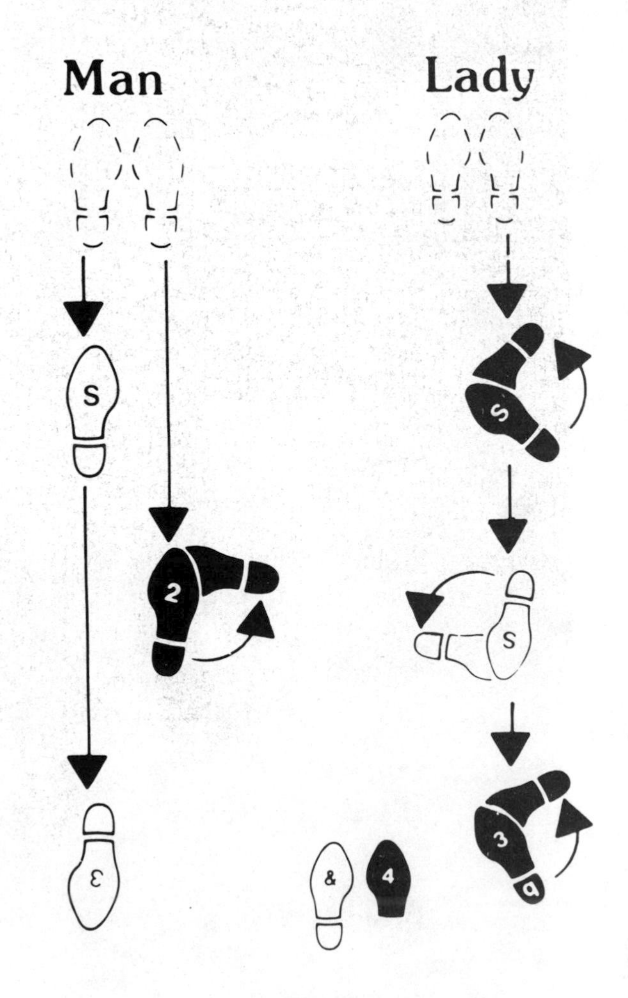

ABBREVIATIONS

Abbreviations are necessary for conserving space, minimizing repetition, and providing a quick reference to dance steps. Following are the abbreviations used to describe dance steps. Capital letters indicate SLOW movements when listed with the step description. Small letters indicate quick movements when written with the step description. Underlined letters when used with parenthesis indicate when the action in parenthesis is to take place.

@	at the same time (indicates the lady's part)
B	Backward (for steps)
B or Bk	Back
Bwd	Backward (for body lead)
Ba-Ch	Ball Change
Cl	Closed or close
Cnt	Contact
X	Cross
Dr	Draw
Fr	Front
F	Forward (for steps)
Fwd	Forward (for body lead)
H	Hands
Ho	Hold
Ki	Kick
L	Left
LOD	Line of dance
M	Man
Meas.	Measure
Q	Quick
R	Right
Sa	Same
Sh	Shoulder
Sd	Sideward or side
S	Slow
T	Turn
2 H	Two-hand position

Glossary

@ At the same time (refers to lady's part). For example, at the same time the man is dancing a cross step, the lady may be dancing an arch step (or some other foot pattern.)

And. A dance call; the indication of the second quick count ("1 and 2 and"); a preparatory signal for starting.

Against line of dance. Clockwise movement aroung the dance floor.

Arch. A partner contact in which they join and raise their hands so that one or both dancers or another couple can go under the raised arms. In full-open position, four contacts are possible: left-right, right-left, right-right, left-left. The arch may be executed while the feet are moving through any of the basic steps.

Ball change. Two changes of weight, on the ball of the foot, from one foot to the other and back.

Ballroom dancing. Dancing that can be done in large ballrooms--foxtrot, rumba, waltz, fun dances, round dances, sequence dances.

Basic steps. Fundamental step patterns; foundation for all other steps.

Break. A change of dance direction, sometimes with a change of rhythm and position. This applies primarily to rhythm dances.

Change of weight. Shifting the weight of the body from the supporting foot to the free foot.

Chasse'. A step and a close, which may be forward or backward but is usually sideward. The free foot never passes the supporting foot. This generally occurs in a series.

Close. (synonym: together): Bringing of feet together and changing weight. The free foot is placed alongside the supporting foot, as in inter-national style.

Contact. Connection of hands between partners. When the instructor indicates contact, he mentions the man's hand first.

Controlled practice. The second phase of teaching a lesson on dancing. Dancers have some freedom in that the instructor tells them (1) what to do but not when to do it or (2) when but not what.

Count. Refers to (1) musical or dance count or (2) the number of weight changes.

Counterbalance. Indicates a change of body direction.

Counterpart. Lady dancing opposite the man but doing the same footwork on opposite feet.

Cross. Moving one foot over the other foot, either forward or backward.

Dance. A particular type and style of step danced to a given piece of music (i.e., foxtrot, rumba, waltz).

Dance rhythm. (1) a repetition of the same sequence of slow and quick movements. For example, the foxtrot contains several well-known rhythms--walk, SSSS; two-step, qqS-qqS; chasse, qqqqqqS-qqqqqqS; box Sqq-Sqq; magic, SSqq; triple magic, SSSqq; (2) a call used to indicate weight changes and used to keep the dancers changing weight rhythmically (i.e., Slow Slow quick quick).

Different. Indicates the lady's foot pattern is different from her partner's.

Direct teaching. The first part of teaching a lesson on dancing. The instructor directs and calls every movement; there is no alternative or free practice.

Double. Both man and lady doing the same step but on opposite feet. "Double" does not mean dancing the step twice.

Draw. After a sideward step, bringing the free foot slowly to the side of the supporting foot, without changing weight, and holding for at least one beat of music.

Figure. One or more steps comprising part of a routine. This may be determined by the phrasing of the music (i.e., sixteen measures equal one phrase, which equal one figure).

Foot movement. Locomotive movement. A foot movement may or may not entail a change of weight: for example, a walking step is a movement with a weight change; a swing or dot of the foot is a movement without a change of weight.

Foot movements and weight changes. There are three basic alternatives relative to music: (1) changing weight once to a beat (slow): (2) changing weight twice to a beat (quick); (3) not changing weight (holding).

Free practice. The third phase of teaching a lesson on dancing. Dancers are free to dance any step in the lesson or routine. Music is playing, but the instructor does not call.

Full turn. A turn in which the dancers make one complete revolution.

Hesitation. A balance step that is held for at least one count.

Hold. (American synonym: dance position): Waiting the designated time before taking another step. The term also is used to describe the additional time that weight is retained on the supporting foot. In International Style--the carriage of the arms, head, and body in relation to one's patner is known as dance position.

In place. Shifting weight without moving feet.

Junior. Indicates a change of position or combining of two positions.

Junior step. Any step requiring a semi-open and reverse position. The lady dances either the same footwork or the same direction as the man; the calls are the same for both sexes.

Kick. Raising the free foot forward, backward, sideward, or crosswise after bending the knee.

Lady same, opposite, or different. Indicates the lady's footwork in relation to the man's.

Lead. The pressure of the man's hand, shoulder, or body to indicate the direction, position, beginning, and end of a movement. To lead, one starts with the left or right foot. The proper lead gets dancers into, through, and out of the step.

Left-left contact. Man's left hand joined with lady's left hand.

Leverage. A body lead indicating a change from a quick to a slow movement, or from a slow to a quick movement, without changing direction.

Line of dance (LOD). Imaginary line counterclockwise around the outside of the room.

Loop, loop turn. Lady turning to the left under the arch; a backward arch turn.

Measure. The portion of music between two bars; it, along with the other measures comprising a given piece of music, consists of a grouping of musical beats containing an equal amount of time.

Movement. Change of foot position. The style or manner of transferring or not transferring weight (axial and/or locomotive).

Music for dancing. The identification of dance rhythms in recorded music is often a real challenge. A few albums have the type of dance printed on the cover or on the label. A very few have the tempo indicated. Both the type of dance and the tempo are of much importance to the dance teacher or the one conducting a dance party. Tempo is indicated by the number of measures per minute.

Music rhythm. Indicates the music beats.

Opposite. Indicates lady's footwork is opposite from that of her partner (her footwork may not be written).

Parenthesis. Indicates further information about the step. The information in parentheses usually (1) does not get a beat of music, (2) does not get a change of weight, (3) may or may not be called by the instructor.

Pivot. Spinning or turning with a partner in closed position without bringing the feet together.

Preparation. Basic or introductory steps that prepare dancers for more advanced steps. Getting ready for a lesson.

Quick. Indicates a change of weight, determined by how long the weight is on the foot. Two quick steps take the same length of time as one slow step, regardless of the tempo of the music.

Right-left contact. Man's right hand joined with lady's left hand.

Right-right contact. Man's right hand joined with lady's left hand.

Rock. Moving back and forth or turning while shifting weight but without changing foot positions.

Routine. One or more figures in a set pattern comprising an entire dance. A routine is the largest subdivision of a dance. Note. You might have an easier time remembering these terms if you think of them in the following manner: the dance can be likened to a completed, written, report; the routine is a paragraph of the report; the figure is a sentence, the step is one word; the unit is a syllable, and the changes of weight (or movement) are letters in the syllable.

Same. Indicates that lady's footwork is the same as her partner's

Senior. Indicates a change of position or combining of two positions (i.e., combining right- and left-side positions).

Senior step. Any step that requires a left- and right-side position, with the lady either traveling in the opposite direction or doing opposite footwork.

Shine or challenge position. Individual position with no contact between partners.

Slow. A slow step. This slow step equals two quick steps and indicates a change of weight.

Spot. Refers to LOD (line of dance) and to the area required for a step that does not progress in any direction but occurs in place.

Step. One or more movements, weight changes, or units. The foot moves in any direction or remains in place. Basic ballroom dance steps are the walk, rock, cross, arch, wheel, pivot, chasse', and hesitation. Basic round dance steps include the hesitation, chug, grapevine, paddle, pas de basque, side ball change, cross ball change, walk, slide, two-step, and swing partner.

Together. Bringing feet together and changing weight, unless otherwise designated.

Touch. Bringing feet together and touching free foot to the floor or to the supporting foot without changing weight.

Unit. One or more movements or changes of weight that comprise a step (i.e., the waltz box consists of two units: first unit--F Sd Cl, second unit--B Sd Cl. In this example, each unit is started on a different foot. The senior walk, magic rhythm, consists of two units: first unit--F F sd cl, second unit--B B sd cl. In this example, each unit is started on the same foot). A step usually consists of one or two units.

Walk. Refers to a dance walk or to extending the free foot beyond the supporting foot; is a progressive alternate transfer of weight from one foot to another during which one foot remains in contact with the floor.

Wheel. Turning around on the spot in positions other than closed, conversation, or shine.

A Special Thanks to all those who helped us show you the dance steps: Jay Osmond, Don Zimmerman, Dana Tueller, Jill Peterson, Zan Peterson, Gayla Coleman.